DATE			

WINNING
STRATEGIES

ROBERT IRWIN
& RITA WOLENIK

WINNING STRATEGIES FOR MANAGING PEOPLE

A TASK DIRECTED
GUIDE

Franklin Watts
New York   Toronto   1985

A *Special Note to the Reader*

There are numerous federal, state, and local laws governing virtually every aspect of labor relations. In addition, laws are constantly being added, changed, and reinterpreted. While this book attempts to explain how to manage given the parameters of the current workplace, it is not intended to be a text on labor-relation legalities or technicalities. Therefore, the reader should not rely on any labor relations material in this book. The authors and the publisher are not involved in providing legal or professional advice. When faced with a labor-relations problem or any legal problem, the reader should seek the advice of a competent legal practitioner.

Library of Congress Cataloging in Publication Data

Irwin, Robert, 1941–
Winning strategies for managing people.

Includes index.
1. Personnel management.   I. Wolenik, Rita.
II. Title.
HF5549.I67   1985   658.3   85-13699
ISBN 0-531-09595-9

CONTENTS

WINNING STRATEGIES

PREFACE

The most successful manager is not the one who does the job fastest. The most successful manager is the one who does the best job.

Yet "lack of time" is the most common complaint heard from managers. As managers, we are constantly looking for ways to go faster. "Look at all the time we'd save," we think, if we could do everything in five-minute or even one-minute spurts of energy.

The trouble is that addressing time directly doesn't really solve much in the real world. *Lack of time isn't the problem.* It's the symptom. Good managers will have plenty of time because of their successful techniques. Poor managers will never have enough no matter how fast they try to go.

Can you imagine the managers at NASA more than a decade ago saying, "What we need is a space shuttle. Now I want each person to take one minute to come up with a way to do it!"

Being quick wasn't nearly as important as being right. The *true* test for the shuttle, after all, was not how fast it was developed, but that it flew.

To build a space shuttle or to hire, fire, and build a good employee involves knowledge of where you're going and understanding of how to get there.

This book gives you both. We will look at the strategies that you as a manager must have in order to manage successfully. More important, we'll break these down into fifteen specific tasks. Each task is really a discrete strategy that you can use to get the specific management result you want. It's important to understand that you can use any of the strategy tasks in this book at any time. You don't have to start at the beginning and work your way through each task in order. If you need to fire someone, look up the tasks on firing. If you need to criticize a worker, see the task labeled criticism. If you need to conduct a hiring interview, see the task on interviewing. You will get instant information on how to solve your immediate problem.

This book is designed to make your job as a manager easier, not to burden you with more things to do. This book will not cost you time, it will save you time.

Once you start using the strategy task approach, you'll find that you are able to move quickly and easily through what otherwise could be difficult, emotion-charged situations. You will suddenly find you have much more time available for accomplishing other tasks.

The goal of this book is to address the source, not the symptom. Its aim is to give you the right answer, when you need it, for the problem you have right now.

TASK 1

HIRING:
OBJECTIVES

*We don't hire people today
to throw them away tomorrow.*

Sign outside a
personnel office

W e've never met a job applicant who didn't want to be successful. But that doesn't mean that every applicant is going to be a success. Many are simply the wrong person for the job. The cost of hiring the wrong person can be great. A hiring mistake will surely reflect badly on you. What's worse, you may end up carrying the person, doing his or her job as well as your own. And ultimately you may not be able to achieve your own work goals because you don't have the support from below.

As a manager, your goal is to hire only the right person. You want to do this with a minimum amount of time, energy and emotional distress. You don't want to spend weeks finding a new employee; that would take too much time away from your own important work. If the next time you need to hire someone you could accomplish the task without fear or anxiety and could do it with great certainty of getting the right person, think of all the energy and time you'd have available to spend on the other important aspects of your job.

The goal of this chapter is to show you how to determine the right person for the job—quickly and easily.

HOW DO YOU FIND
THE RIGHT PERSON?

We once knew a manager who had a quick hiring method. He hired the first person who responded to his job advertisement regardless of who that person was. He swore that it didn't matter, that he could take anyone— anyone at all—and with six months of training have that person successfully doing any job!

There's probably a lot more truth to that conviction than most managers would care to admit! And it's unlikely that many would put it into practice. The risk of getting the wrong person is too great. When hiring, most people are going to do everything possible to get just the right person for the job.

But exactly how is that done? Most managers don't have a *person strategy*. So they come up with an often ill-conceived plan thought up on the spur of the moment.

A SPUR-OF-THE-MOMENT PLAN

Has this ever happened to you? Suddenly you need to hire someone. Your first thoughts are these:

1. With all the work I have to do, now I have the job of hiring someone on top of it. (Dislike)

2. If I don't hire the right person for the job, the result will reflect negatively on my abilities as a manager. (Fear)

3. I'll have to get started right away. I'll need to write a job description and put an ad in the paper, then I'll need to read resumes and then I'll have to interview. My God, how will I get everything done? (Scrambling)

Most managers improvise a plan each time they need to hire. That, however, is not the best way—or even a satisfactory way—of doing it. The results can be most dissatisfying. You can end up with a person who really wants to do something else, who took your job to fill in until the right job comes along. Perhaps your new employee really wants to be a singer. She gives you only part-time energy and part-time dedication while working full-time toward her chosen career.

Or perhaps your new worker really wants to be out in the field selling or interviewing. But he's taken a desk job because he needed work right away and that's all that was available. He may try to do good work, but with his heart outside, he isn't going to be able to produce the kind of enthusiasm and energy you may demand.

GETTING THE RIGHT PERSON

To get the right person for the job, you need to know exactly what the person's own goals are. You need to know that the person is operating on the same wavelength you are, and really wants to do the work the job offers. This means not only having a job description (which we'll get to in the next chapter) but also a "person description." This is both easier and harder than it sounds. It's easier because creating a person description is fairly simple. It's harder because most people tend to forget to use such a description even when they have it.

Therefore, to begin, you need to have a "person objectives" strategy. You set down your goals for the person you hire. You put it aside and have it ready. Whenever you need to hire, you whip out your goals and modify them, if necessary, to the particular job. There's no worry, no fear, and no wasted time. You don't need to scramble. You just look at your objectives and find the person who fits.

DEFINING YOUR "PERSON OBJECTIVES"

Each time you hire, you must remember that hiring is part of a long-term process. The danger is that you will consider only your goals of the moment. Typically you need someone right now who's willing to do the work and is pleasant to be around.

You must realize that hiring isn't just a single, unrelated incident in your work day. It is part of a process that involves the entire term of employment. It's a process that involves a *long-term* relationship.

We don't hire people today to throw them away tomorrow. When you hire today, your objective is success six months, a year, three years, five years, or longer down the road. You're hiring for the future as well as for the present.

Once you remember you're involved in a long-term process, you can define your long- and short-term objectives for the person you're hiring.

PERSON DESCRIPTION

Short-term objectives typically are such things as:

1. Someone who'll take the job right away.
2. Someone with at least minimum experience.
3. Someone who can communicate with me.

You undoubtedly have your own short-term objectives to add to this list.

Long-term objectives, on the other hand, are quite different. The employee may not be able to achieve these today. The question is will he or she be able to achieve them during the full course of employment?

Typical long-term employee objectives are:

1. *Results.* The employee will work on a specific project and satisfactorily complete it in a specific time.
2. *Independence.* The employee will be able to work (a) independently (b) with little supervision (c) with moderate supervision.

3. *Work habits*. The employee will "get along" and work as part of a team.

4. *Dedication*. The employee will demonstrate dedication by applying discipline, creativity, and whatever talents he or she may have to the job. The employee will also give "quality time" and energy to the job.

5. *Motivation*. The employee will be enthusiastic, ready to meet the job's challenge.

6. *Loyalty*. The employee will support me, the company, and the project.

Your objectives may be different (but probably not much different) from these, and you may have additional ones. What's important to remember, however, is that you need to define your goals for the person you are going to hire. If you don't first set objectives for the person you're looking for, how will you recognize your new employee when you see him or her?

Hint: All of these objectives are really specific ways of stating the general objective that the employee will make a strong commitment to the job. It doesn't matter whether the employee is going to be selling french fries at a lunch counter or making multi-million dollar loans at a bank. During the time the employee is working for you, what you want is commitment to the job. The trick, of course, is to identify commitment.

THE BUILDING BLOCKS OF HIRING

Once you know what your hiring goals for the person are, how do you determine whether or not an applicant fits those goals?

Hiring is not a single act. It requires making a series of decisions, one depending on the other. There is a job description to write, applicants to recruit, resumes to read, and interviews to conduct. You've done the first, but important, step: you've determined who you are looking for. The rest of hiring is trying to find that person.

Finding the right person, even if you know what you want, can still seem overwhelming if you try to tackle the whole thing at once. It's like trying to eat a whole pie; your stomach would surely balk. However, if you cut it up into smaller slices and then eat each slice separately over a period of time, not only will you finish the pie, but you'll enjoy it, too!

The next chapters cover each of the tasks involved in hiring and show you how to accomplish them quickly and easily.

The first step, however, is knowing who you are looking for. Once you have your "person objectives" in hand, you'll feel much more comfortable about making hiring decisions.

TASK 2

HIRING: JOB DESCRIPTION AND RECRUITING

Let us describe the undescribable!

paraphrased from
Childe Harold's Pilgrimage,
Canto IV, Byron

In order to recruit applicants you must be able to describe the job you are offering. Hence, it's only natural to include both of these under the same task. We will, however, cover them separately—first writing the job description, then using it to recruit.

WRITING THE JOB DESCRIPTION

Written job descriptions are used for classified ads, bulletin boards, employment agencies, in fact for almost any source you have, including the applicants themselves. People who are looking for jobs need to know what you are offering. You tell them in the job description. That's why they are so important. They are not hard to write and can be done in a matter of a few minutes. Before we go into the technique of writing them, there are two areas to consider:

1. Remember that this is a *job* description, not an applicant description. Applicant descriptions are something you keep in mind as you go through the steps of hiring (see Task 1) The goal here is to get an applicant who is qualified for the *job*. By the time you begin interviewing, every applicant you see should minimally qualify for the position you're trying to fill.

2. The job description should avoid any hint of discrimination. That means it must not discriminate against any protected category. (See Task 5.)

THE ACTUAL DESCRIPTION

Always think of a job description as having *two* parts. In the first part, you describe what the employee will do *on the job*. In the second part, you describe the requirements the employee must have for doing it. The easiest way to accomplish this is to divide a page down the middle with a line. On the left side indicate what the employee will do. On the right, list the requirement for doing it.

For example, if you are hiring someone to deliver express packages, the left side of the sheet will read:

Will handle
delivery route

Now put the requirements for handling a delivery route on the right side:

Must have
a commercial
driver's license

You start on the left and just describe what the person will do in the job. Then you figure out what a requirement for that might be. Everything that a person does on the job has some sort of requirement. For example, perhaps you're looking for a copy editor for a house journal. The sheet might read:

Will write	*Must have a BA*
and edit copy	*degree in English*
	and be able to
	spell accurately

Or you might be hiring a cashier:

Will work on	*Must be bondable*
cash register in	
retail outlet	

Or maybe you need a salesperson:

Will handle	*Must have prior*
over-the-counter	*sales experience*
sales of	*in field*
feminine products	*with feminine*
	merchandise

When you've listed a complete description of what the person will do "on the job" on the left side and a complete set of requirements "for the job" on the right side, simply put together all the items on the left side as a first paragraph and all the items on the right side as a second paragraph and you have a comprehensive, detailed, and accurate job description ready to use.

Hint: Items that are done "on the job" usually start with "will." The applicant *will* do this or that. Items that are requirements usually start with "must". Applicant *must* have this or that.

RECRUITING

Recruiting is a critical part of hiring and should not be left to anyone but yourself. Remember, the employee you finally hire will come from the pool of applicants you use.

There are many sources of applicants. They are listed here in terms of those we have found to be most promising to least promising.

SOURCES OF APPLICANTS

1. *Referrals* from other people you know in the business. Posting on bulletin boards within the company can

also be a source here. Some companies pay a bonus to employees for successful referrals. (There could be a potential anti-discrimination problem here unless the job is also widely advertised and open competition for it is held.)

2. *Rehiring* former employees with proven records. Some companies keep track of former employees for just this purpose.

3. *Promotion* from inside the company, as long as you provide proper training. (It's important not to get trapped into promoting just on the basis of seniority; you could end up with the wrong person for the job.)

4. *Weekend Open Houses* are particularly useful in a tight labor market where many companies are competing for the same type of employee. (This is frequently the case in high-tech and aerospace companies.)

5. *Classified Advertising* in papers likely to be read by potential employees (This is costly, but it does get the news out that you're looking for someone.)

6. *Stealing* by using "head hunters" to hire from your competitors. (This is very costly and there is the danger that the person you hire may be the person your competitor was just getting ready to fire.)

7. *Employment Agencies*—not the head hunters, but the kind where the employee pays the fee. The trouble here is that they will usually send everyone over who's warm. This can be a good source for lower-paying jobs, however, if you get to know someone you can trust in the agency.

8. *Unions and School Placement Offices.* Depending on the job both these sources will provide applicants.

9. *State Employment Offices.* The applicants here sometimes really don't want the job!

10. *Application File.* You call up personnel and ask, "Who do we have on file for such-and-such a job." You usually get an indiscriminate list of names as a response.

To find the *top* applicants you may need to start at the beginning of the list and work through to the end. A lot depends on luck, on the time you have available, and on the contacts you've established.

TASK 3

HIRING: SCREENING RESUMES AND/OR JOB APPLICATIONS FOR "POP-UPS"

When you see a fig in a bowl of cherries, you know you've got a problem.

Personnel Manager's observation

Many managers complain that they just don't have time to read through resumes and/or job application forms. That's probably because they don't know what they are reading them for. You can read a large stack of these in thirty minutes or less, *if* you know what to look for.

It's important to understand that resumes and/or applications are more negative than positive. While it's true that you normally look for something in them that will make you want to interview the applicant, it's more likely that you are looking for something that will allow you to *eliminate* the person. Typically, you may have several dozen applicants, but you want to conduct only half a dozen interviews or less. The resume and/or application thus becomes a device for separating the chaff from the wheat. It lets you cull out those who you think can't handle the job.

If that's the case, then you must be very good at your reading. If you're careless, or if you delegate the reading to others, you just might find yourself throwing out the very best candidates and interviewing the less desirable ones.

POP-UPS

When reading resumes and/or applications there are certain items to watch out for. We call these "pop-ups" because they often pop up out of the background of what's written.

If you know what these pop-ups are, you can scan a resume and/or application for them quickly and in just a few moments make a decision on whether or not to interview.

POP-UP 1:
DIRECTION

Read the part of the resume that shows previous work experience over the past ten years. Has the applicant been moving toward the kind of work you have to offer? Or has the movement been in the other direction? You don't want to hire someone whose mind lies elsewhere.

Another area to check is hobbies and clubs, if listed. Do they fit in with the kind of work you want the person to do? A person whose hobby is skiing might not be right for you if your busy season is winter weekends. Yet another item to look for is "stature." Has the person's previous work experience been appropriate to the stature of the job you offer? (If it has been higher, the applicant may feel this job is a step down.)

Finally, look for "achievements." In this world there are "doers" and there are "wheel spinners." Does the applicant list any awards, prizes, or recognitions of accomplishments to show that they know how to get things done?

POP-UP 2:
MULTIPLES

The single best indicator of how the applicant will perform working for you is how he or she performed working for someone else. Look at work history. If the applicant has had a strong work history, there's every reason to think he or she will continue to be a strong worker.

The question, of course, is how do you know from the application? One good way is to check for "multiples." Multiples means that the applicant has either had multiple jobs over his or her work history *or* has had multiple duties within jobs. The best candidates usually have had *both*.

You can check multiple jobs by counting the *number* of past employers that the applicant has had. Many seasoned personnel people feel that the ideal candidate will have changed companies every three to four years. More often than that can mean a problem either in getting along with others or in work performance. Longer than five years in a job can mean the applicant is too set in his or her ways to adapt easily to new company demands.

Multiple *duties* are revealed by what the applicant has written with regard to "responsibilities" or "duties" on past jobs. (Every resume should include this information.) Look for an applicant who has had many different duties and responsibilities. The *variety* indicates competence, the ability to learn and, most important, that others have trusted the individual to move to increasing responsibilities.

This technique can be difficult to apply to younger applicants, particularly those just out of school. Nevertheless, you can look for multiples in school performance; extracurricular activities, outside interests, part-time jobs all indicate a positive and highly motivated person.

POP-UP 3:
SALARY PROGRESSION

A person who has multiples should also show a steady upward movement in salary. In business, the rewards of good work are monetary. The pop-up here is when the applicant *fails to show or leaves out* salary progression. If he or she has not gotten an increase in salary over the years, then there is usually a good reason why the rewards of hard work have been denied.

POP-UP 4:
DATE GAPS

A good resume should give work history from the time the applicant left school or at least for the past ten years. In a normal resume this means *every bit of time.* If there is a gap between one job and the next, it is important to know why.

It can be for reasons as innocuous as going back to school or taking time out to raise children. Or it could be that the applicant was unemployable during that period. Was he or she in jail? In a mental institution? Fighting bankruptcy proceedings?

Good applicants will usually make sure that every bit of their time is accounted for. They don't want you to think the worst.

POP-UP 5:
AMBIGUITIES

There's an old saying that goes, "If you can't dazzle them with brilliance, baffle them with bullshit." An applicant who has had successful job experiences should have no trouble clearly stating those experiences. On the other hand, an applicant who wants to hide a bad job history or a problem may rely on ambiguities. In describing "responsibilities" in a previous job, the applicant writes, "In charge of multiple office operations." Really? Does that mean he or she made coffee as well as ran the mail room?

Applicants who have something to hide and who do

not lie, will often use ambiguities on the theory that it's up to the employer to figure out what's meant. If the resume is ambiguous, a good rule of thumb is to assume there's a problem.

Another place this often occurs is when the application asks, "Reason for leaving job," the applicant may write "better job offer." Indeed? Does the next job the applicant lists show increased responsibilities or higher salary? If not, how was it a better job offer? Remember, an ambiguous answer often is a cover-up for a problem.

FOLLOW UP: LYING

These are items to check after you've selected those resumes/applications of applicants you think you might want to interview.

There are no degrees to lying. Either something is the truth or it's a lie. One lie on an application should be enough to dump the applicant. (If the person lies on the application, what will they do on the job?)

Typical places for spotting lies are *starting and ending salaries*. The applicant knows exactly what salary he or she started at and ended at or can quickly find out. Exaggerated claims here are just lies. These *sometimes* can be verified through reference checks.

Another place where applicants sometimes lie is explaining why they left a company. An applicant may give one reason, but if you run a simple credit check it may turn up a bankruptcy or other problem. (Note: You may need to get permission from the applicant to run the check.)

Yet another area for lying has to do with education. Applicants may exaggerate college degrees. A letter to the college registrar's office can be very revealing. (You may need to wait until you've hired the applicant before you can check with the college unless having a degree is a specific job requirement.)

Reading a resume is really a job of elimination. If you know the pop-ups to look for, usually you can very quickly eliminate those applicants who aren't right for the job.

TASK 4

HIRING: GETTING HONEST ANSWERS FROM REFERENCES

Never give a sucker
An even break!

W.C. Fields

There was a time not long ago when a prospective employer could call an applicant's former boss or associate and ask, "Did Marc have any problems at work," or, "Why did you fire Jill from that job," and expect to get reasonably straightforward answers.

That, however, was before the recent wave of litigation in which employees sue former employers or associates for giving bad or "false" references. Today most employers are gun-shy. If you call asking for a reference, chances are you'll get an answer such as, "We don't respond to verbal requests for references." When you send a written request, you may get no response at all. Rather than take a chance on a lawsuit, they'd rather not say anything. Or if they do respond, it's by replying to *all* inquiries in a positive way, disguising true feelings.

There are two exceptions to this. The first is where the old employer goes out of the way to give a marvelous letter of recommendation to a terminating employee. The applicant shows you the letter, you call, and the old boss repeats everything in the letter. Chances are the only way the former employer could get rid of this employee was by issuing such a letter. He or she is just tickled pink you are going to get this employee off his or her back.

The other exception to this is the "plant". This is a friend of the former employee at the old job. On the application the applicant has listed the name of a person to call in the old company. You call, and this "plant" just bubbles over with information about the applicant.

GETTING HONEST ANSWERS

If you're hiring and you want honest references, how do you get them in an age of deception?

The answer is that you have to have a few tricks of your own.

When checking references be sure to first get permission from the applicant to contact those listed as references.

RULE 1:
NEVER SAY YOU'RE
CHECKING A REFERENCE

If you call and say you're checking a reference, any alert employer or manager will immediately be on guard. He or she will know better than to say anything derogatory, perhaps they will not be willing to say anything at all. Thus if you call saying you're conducting a reference check, the answer probably is already "No!"

Therefore, if you can't get information the direct way by saying you're checking a reference, you have to do it indirectly. Always begin by asking for the applicant's old boss (direct superior). Don't call personnel; they've been trained to tell you nothing.

When you call, say you only want to know if the applicant used to work there. A phrase such as, "verifying former employment" usually works well. (Lots of people call for this reason—from banks to credit-checking companies.) Chances are even the most gun-shy manager or employer will be willing to answer such an innocuous question.

RULE 2:
ESTABLISH RAPPORT

If you get an affirmative answer to your first question, try to strike up a conversation with the former boss. What product is made or service offered by the company? What is its correct address? Just ask simple questions that you could find out from the telephone book. Don't hint that what the former boss says is going to be used to make a hiring decision.

If the former boss seems to want to talk, yet is hesitant, don't assume it's the questions you're asking. You don't know who may be in earshot of the conversation at the other end. Maybe he or she feels uncomfortable discussing the former employee at that moment. Ask if you can call back later, or at a different phone. *Don't* ask if you can call the former boss's home unless he or she suggests it.

RULE 3:
NEVER ASK
LEADING QUESTIONS

Don't ask the former boss to give you his or her impression of the employee. Don't ask if the employee had any problems. Don't ask about weaknesses. These will immediately put the former boss on guard. Remember, he or she can simply hang up on you at any time.

Instead ask if the former boss will *verify* what the applicant has already told you. The boss only has to answer "yes" or "no" to questions about what the former employee did, not their performance. Now read off the description given by the applicant of his or her former job. (You may want to especially consider duties that you think the applicant will need to perform on the current job). Snickers or long pauses here can tell you a lot.

Finally, if you've established good rapport, the former boss may volunteer some insights into the past employee. If the boss mentions that the employee was "particularly good" at this or that, it could mean that the applicant was "not particularly good" at things not praised.

USING OTHER SOURCES

THE "OLD BOY" SYSTEM

Another very productive fount of information on applicants can be your own contacts. If you're an engineer from MIT or Berkeley, for example, and you have an applicant from a company which might itself have an engineer from your school, you might give your old school "chum" a call. Even if you've never met the person, the fact that you went to the same school can sometimes be enough of a bond to allow you to get the "lowdown" on an applicant (particularly if it turns out you and your "chum" belonged to the same fraternity, sorority, club, etc.). If you can establish rapport with the school "chum," you might work the conversation around to something like, "I'm trying to hire this person, but it's my neck if he/she doesn't work out. Is there any way you can find out if this person's okay or if he/she had any problems?"

This is called "networking." The "Old Boy" system works particularly well for military personnel, fraternity and sorority members, or any other group that feels any sort of continuing allegiance among its members.

COUNTERPART CONTACT

Another good source to contact is the person who has the same title as you. If you're purchasing manager, contact the purchasing manager at the applicant's old employer. If you're in accounts receivable, contact the accounts receivable person. Start talking about the job. Chances are the other person will realize your problems are just like his or hers and may open up with vital information about the applicant.

TASK 5

HIRING: CONDUCT MEANINGFUL INTERVIEWS

Listen. Listen. Listen.

The three rules
of interviewing

The hiring decision is usually based upon the interview. You know it and the applicant knows it. Because so much depends on the interview, it can be a tension-filled meeting in which the applicant strives mightily to present the best possible image while you strive just as mightily to strip away the applicant's "front." This kind of situation, with both parties "on guard," is not ideally suited to communication.

It would be a mistake to anticipate that in every interview you will get the applicant to "open up" and reveal all. Nevertheless, it is still possible to conduct highly revealing interviews provided you approach them with a specific strategy and with clear goals in mind. This can be accomplished if the interview process is broken down into six minitasks:

Minitask 1: Determine your interview goals
Minitask 2: Develop an interview style
Minitask 3: Understand the applicant
Minitask 4: Plan the interview
Minitask 5: Prepare specific questions
Minitask 6: Know what to look and listen for

MINITASK 1:
YOUR GOALS

Before doing any interviewing, you need to be very clear about what your goals are, about what you want to get out of the interview. Obviously, you want to check on the *knowledge* and *skills* of the applicant. You want to find out what he or she is able to do.

Interviewers who *only* focus on knowledge and abilities, however, often miss out on the most important information available from an interview, namely, *what kind of person* is sitting across the table. (See Task 1.)

You also need to know if the applicant will be committed to the job, if he or she will bring along energy and enthusiasm. Remember, an applicant who has the knowledge and ability to do a job, but who isn't committed to it makes a far worse employee than an applicant who doesn't know anything, but is committed enough to study day and night to learn the skills needed to do the work. Interviewing for knowledge and abilities is one thing. Interviewing for commitment is something else entirely. To get the right employee, you need to do both.

MINITASK 2: DEVELOP AN INTERVIEW STYLE

There are several different methods of conducting interviews which have become popular lately. Each is strategically aimed at getting the applicant to reveal as much as possible about knowledge and abilities as well as about personality.

THE RAPPORT INTERVIEW

This interview rarely lasts more than fifty minutes (about the same amount of time a person would spend in a psychiatrist's office). The idea is to follow a psychoanalytical approach in which the applicant is led to deeper and deeper levels of communication, and, along the way reveals all.

The technique is based on rapport. The interviewer must quickly establish friendly communication with the applicant on a person-to-person basis. Once this is done, the interviewer honestly reveals one of his or her own minor personality traits. Because of the rapport that has already been established, the applicant now feels obliged to be equally revealing about a minor trait. Feelings of honesty, communication, and bond between the two people increase. Now the interviewer honestly reveals another bit of knowledge, ability, or personality trait that he or she has, and the applicant is encouraged to follow suit.

It could be described as "opening up". The interviewer takes off his coat and hangs it up. The applicant feels uncomfortable sitting there with a coat on, so he takes his off as well. The interviewer loosens his tie. The applicant relaxes and does likewise.

Obviously, it only goes so far and the applicant eventually refuses to "completely undress" or completely reveal himself at some level. However, a skilled interviewer can use this technique to get enormous insights into the applicant in just a short period of time.

What works against this technique is the situation of the interview. Rapport requires calm and relaxation. An interview, on the other hand, is frequently frought with tension. To overcome this some managers conduct this kind of an interview in a lounge situation, in easy chairs, or sitting next to the applicant on a couch. Going out to lunch with an applicant can be useful where appropriate.

A word of warning, however. You can't conduct a rapport interview unless you really know yourself. You have to be willing to be really open about your own personality, knowledge, and abilities. No fudging! An applicant can tell in an instant if you aren't being honest and the effect is spoiled.

The biggest problem with this kind of interview is

that it emphasizes learning about the personality of the applicant. You can often quickly determine the person's commitment to a job. On the other hand, it is less useful in revealing an applicant's knowledge and skills for a job.

THE MULTIPLE INTERVIEW

This interviewing technique is literally based on exhaustion. There isn't one single interview. Rather there are three, four, or five interviews of the applicant—one right after the other.

Typically, an applicant is asked to report for an interview at 9:00 in the morning and is told the interview might last for several hours. He or she is then interviewed for about an hour by either someone from personnel or a boss who will not be the applicant's direct superior (if hired) but who will work with him or her in an associate position. The applicant is not told there will be other interviews.

When this first interview ends, the applicant is introduced by the interviewer to the person who will be his or her immediate supervisor in the job and another hour interview is held. Again, the applicant is not told there will be other interviews.

At the end of this session, the applicant is introduced by the interviewer to a more superior boss and an additional hour's interview is held. Finally, this interviewer introduces the applicant to the division head, or some other higher-ranking supervisor, who takes the applicant out to lunch and there conducts a final interview.

The strategy has two distinct advantages. If any interviewer along the way feels the applicant will not qualify, he or she can end the process and eliminate the person by not progressing to the next step. The interview is ended cordially and the applicant never knows there were other interview hurdles to overcome. If the applicant does make it to the final stage, he or she has passed through the gauntlet and the top boss can make a job offer on the spot. Alternatively, the four interviewers can get together and compare notes before making a hiring decision.

The second advantage of the strategy is that four consecutive interviews (each of which covers much of the same material) practically forces the applicant to reveal his or her true self. Weaknesses will pop out somewhere along the way, as will true personality traits. The applicant will be driven to self-revelation out of sheer exhaustion. It's the same technique that is often used by the police when questioning a suspect. The suspect must repeat his or her story over and over again to different people. When those people compare notes, inconsistencies glaringly stand out.

The problem with the multiple technique is that it is both time- and personnel-consuming. Three or more interviewers are required for each applicant. Therefore, it is used mostly for high-level positions.

STRESS INTERVIEWING

This technique became popular a few years back when several high-level managers revealed that it was their method of identifying weaknesses in potential employees. In one case, a manager purposely cut half an inch off one leg of the chair in which the applicant sat for the interview. While the interviewer sat steadily watching from a large, comfortable seat, the applicant wobbled on a fragile wooden chair. This tended to distract and embarrass the applicant. The result was that applicants who had prepared themselves with "cover stories" frequently forgot them, became confused, and in the process revealed their true personalities and job weaknesses.

Another boss would change the lighting in the room where the interview was conducted. She placed her desk in front of a large window from which the curtains had been removed. In addition, bright lights behind her were turned on. The effect was that while she could see easily, the applicant was blinded by the lighting and had trouble looking at her. Again the result was that the applicant felt distracted and tended to make revealing mistakes.

This technique relies on increasing the natural tension that occurs during an interview to the point where the applicant "breaks" and reveals all. In some cases it is amazingly efficient, particularly where the job requires the employee to work under great stress. It does, however, have two drawbacks. Some applicants simply fall apart in such a situation, yet would make excellent employees. They end up talking gibberish, feeling foolish, and refusing to take the job even if it is offered.

On the other hand, there are some clever applicants who immediately understand what's happening and turn the situation around by commenting on the bad chair or the poor lighting and ultimately embarrassing the interviewer.

It isn't necessary that you use one technique only. You can borrow some aspects from various methods, using those which work best for you. In the end, you'll probably end up simply asking questions and hoping for the best. Nevertheless, if you keep these techniques in the back of your mind, they may give you a little edge over the applicant.

MINITASK 3:
UNDERSTAND THE APPLICANT

In today's marketplace, a manager must assume that the applicant is savvy to interviewing techniques. Many applicants even pay for coaching on how to handle interviewers. Most applicants regard getting a job as a kind of war in which the interview is the biggest battle. They come ready for it and unless you, as interviewer, are aware of what's going on, you can get blown right out of the water.

TURNING THE TABLES

The first thing that applicants are taught is to turn the tables on the interviewer. As soon as the interview starts, an applicant using this technique begins asking you questions about the company and about yourself. As you answer, they probe deeper and deeper, continually nodding approval and smiling as you answer. You have the feeling that things are going well. Soon an hour has passed and you realize you've spent the entire time talking about yourself and the company. You haven't really learned much about the applicant, but you feel you really do like the person and would therefore like to give them the job.

You've been had. These applicants know that the quickest way to make another person like them is to listen to that person talk. They've gotten you to talk and they've listened. They've become your friend, your confidant. Maybe you've revealed a couple of problems and they've been sympathetic. Who wouldn't like such an applicant!

What they've done is to turn the tables. Instead of you interviewing them, they've interviewed you. If they want the job, their nodding and smiling tells you you've passed and they're more than halfway to their goal of getting hired.

HOW TO KEEP THE TABLES
FROM GETTING TURNED

A few years ago, when applicants were unsophisticated, this wasn't much of a problem. But today, applicants at all levels know this technique and managers must be on guard against it. The way to avoid the problem is to recognize the fact that we get information by *listening*, not by talking.

Often this is hardest when an applicant asks you about the company right at the beginning of the interview. Yes, you will need to tell the applicant about the company, but usually not until the *end* of the interview. Until then you don't need to. A good rule of thumb when interviewing is to speak 10 percent of the time and listen 90 percent of the time. One manager we know has a special way of getting himself ready for an interview. He goes into a corner and repeats to himself, "Listen! Listen! Listen!" Then he's ready to interview.

If the applicant asks a question, you can give a brief reply which ends with another question. As we'll see shortly, you can lead into questions that require long, thought-out answers. As long as you follow the principle of listening, not talking, the applicant can't turn the tables on you.

SPILLING THE BEANS

Applicants have also learned that the way to get hired is to tell the interviewer what he or she wants to hear. Therefore, today's modern applicant almost invariably will begin by asking you, "What is the job you want me to do?" This seems a reasonable enough question. After all, how can you expect a person to interview for a position if they don't know what it is?

So you explain the responsibilities of the position. Along the way the applicant asks some specific questions about what the employee is supposed to do and how he or she will be expected to act. After five minutes or so the applicant nods that he or she understands what the job is and now you begin the formal interview. Even if you follow the 90/10 rule about listening and not talking, you find that this applicant is exactly what you want. It's incredible. The applicant's background and personality fits perfectly with the job. How can you not hire the person?

You've been had, again. The applicant began by finding out what kind of a person you were looking for, then molded his or her background and personality to fit that person. You can be certain if you tell someone what you want, they will quickly become that person. The minute you let them know that vital information, you've "spilled the beans" and you might as well forget the rest of the interview.

HOW TO KEEP THE BEANS IN THE PAN

When applicants ask what the job is, they are really asking, "What kind of a person are you looking for?" Don't tell them.

You're conducting the interview and you have options. You can simply ignore the question and refuse to answer it. If that seems rude or inappropriate, you can hand over a copy of the formal job description and give the applicant a few moments to read it. If the applicant asks questions about it, you can simply say, "The description is comprehensive. The job is exactly what's written there, no more, no less. Now let's discuss your background." Another strategy when the applicant asks about the job is to turn the question around. Reply by asking, "What do you think the job is?" When the applicant replies you can then say, "That's pretty close, now let's get on with the interview."

Remember, *never reveal the kind of person you're looking for beforehand.*

MINITASK 4:
PLAN THE INTERVIEW

There are many different ways of actually planning the interview. However, we have developed a four-step procedure that works best in getting the applicant to reveal information about knowledge, abilities, and potential commitment.

1. Establish rapport
2. Go over the applicant's job history
3. Describe job being offered
4. Chat and close

ESTABLISH RAPPORT

To learn about the real person you must get beyond the superficial ritual of small talk, you must get the applicant to lower his or her defenses, to open up, to tell you who and what they really are. For some people, this is very easy; for others, it is incredibly difficult.

Rapport is not just a fancy word. It's an important description that means "intimate human contact". It's not physical contact, but sympathetic person-to-person communication which some have described as psychological or even spiritual. Some call it "rapping" and others "breaking through." Whatever you call it, it means becoming intimate enough with another person so that they feel comfortable telling you information about themselves.

There are a few people who go through their whole lives never establishing true rapport with others. Yet it's not hard to accomplish. All that's necessary is first, to show the other person that you care about them and second, to open yourself up so they can see who you really are.

In the context of an employment interview, showing you care may mean asking if the person had any trouble in finding the interview location. Do they need a parking validation? Are they feeling up to an interview? Have they had a good day so far? Did they get a good night's sleep? Another more direct method is to carefully explain the interview process: that you will ask questions so you can learn about the other person, that you will take notes so you can be sure to remember what was said, that you want to give the other person every opportunity to express themselves and to be comfortable about what they say. It's mostly a matter of putting yourself in the other person's shoes so you'll get a feeling for what they're concerned about, and then being sympathetic.

Opening up can mean an amiable conversation during which you might share one part of your life, perhaps some one experience that happened to you that day. It could be your opinion of a song or sport report you heard on the radio on the way to work; it could be a conversation you had with the kid down in the snack bar; it could be a revelation about the universe that came to you. The only critical thing is that it be revealing of yourself as a person.

Try some of these techniques the next time you meet anyone for the first time. It may take a few attempts before you get it right, but most people who are honest about themselves and who do honestly care about others can establish good rapport in less than five minutes with anyone they are meeting for the first time!

GO OVER THE
APPLICANT'S JOB HISTORY

A good way to start is to briefly begin with the applicant's education and quickly move to job history. This is where you can check for knowledge and skills as well as get a feeling for the person's ability to commit to a job. If you noticed any gaps or other pop-ups in the application, ask about them here.

When trying to learn about the applicant's knowledge, one manager we know uses an unusual technique: He *uses wrong information to get the right answer.*

While going over the applicant's job history, Perry would try to think about what he knew of the applicant's expertise. Almost always Perry could find some little bit of information he had tucked away about what the applicant had done, some part of what the applicant surely must know if that person indeed had the skills and knowledge claimed.

Perry would then take that fact he knew was correct and state it *incorrectly* to the applicant. If the applicant knew the subject, he or she would usually correct Perry politely. If the applicant didn't correct him, Perry would try to be sure the applicant had heard what had been said. He would repeat the *incorrect* statement asking, "That's right, isn't it?"

If the applicant now agreed, Perry knew one of two things. Either the person didn't know what they were supposed to know *or* they were too shy to correct the potential boss's error. Either way, Perry would seriously consider eliminating the person.

Perry once was hiring an artist to do layouts for the company's annual report. He said, "I'd like to use a serif type like Helvetica." ("Serif" means a type style that has a cursive look to it. Any layout artist worth his salt knows that Helvetica is a *sans* serif type or one *without* serifs.) When the artist nodded agreement, Perry immediately knew the man was a fraud.

DESCRIBE THE JOB
BEING OFFERED

This should be done *only* at the end of the interview. Often there is a game played at this point to try to find out the lowest salary the applicant will accept. The applicant, on the other hand, will try to keep from telling you this vital information if at all possible, and instead tries to find out the highest possible salary that you will pay.

If the game appeals to you, there are some phrases which can be helpful, such as, "Are you anticipating a salary higher than your last job? How much higher?" Or, "Give me a ball-park figure for what it would take to make you comfortable here."

However, we have found that it works better to simply give a salary range for the job and then negotiate the actual salary, if necessary, once we've decided which applicant to accept. (It's important not to be penny wise and pound foolish. You don't necessarily want to hire the cheapest applicant—you want the best.)

CHAT AND CLOSE

The interview begins when you meet the applicant and ends when he or she leaves. *All* the rest of the time is interview. Chatting casually after the formal interview has ended can often be the most revealing part. The applicant may now feel that the interview hurdle is over, and will relax and open up. You may learn more in five minutes of chatting than you did in sixty minutes of interviewing.

MINITASK 5: PREPARE SPECIFIC QUESTIONS

It's a good idea to have a number of questions to ask written out in advance and an equally good idea to write down the answers the applicant gives. If you explain at the beginning of the interview that you will be taking notes to help you remember what the applicant says, there shouldn't be any objection.

QUESTIONS YOU MUST NOT ASK

There are a number of items you must be careful not to ask about in interviewing. They include, but are not limited to, questions about the following protected categories:

Race
Religion
Color

Sex
National Origin
Age (over 40)
Veteran Status (particularly Vietnam)
Handicap (including in some cases cancer)

Even questions which remotely relate to these areas should not be asked. For example, a question such as, "Does your religion allow you to work on Saturdays?" might be a violation. It would be better to phrase the question, "The job requires Saturday work. Will you be able to do that?"

(*Note:* Some protections are national, such as those covering race, religion, and color. Some vary by state, such as those covering marital status. The rules covering discrimination are quite extensive and ever-changing. A detailed examination of them is beyond the scope of this book. When hiring, you should check with state or local employment bureaus or your own personnel department, or consult with a labor-relations specialist (preferably an attorney) to determine the laws currently applicable in your particular situation.)

QUESTIONS TO ASK

TRAINABILITY

"What jobs have you had which required specific training?"

"Tell me about the kinds of equipment (typewriters, machines, etc.) you've worked on."

"What kind of training would you like us to give you in this job?"

FLEXIBILITY AND STATURE

"How would you handle working for two bosses?"

"If someone came to you with a complaint on the job, how would you handle it?"

PAST WORK EXPERIENCE

"When we call your previous employers for references, what do you think they will tell us? Please explain."

PERSONAL OUTLOOK

"Describe what you expect to be doing during a typical day on the job."

"If you could have been the boss in your last job, what things would you have changed?"

"What is your biggest concern in taking this job?"

LONG-TERM OUTLOOK

"Describe a day on the job two years from now."

"When you retire at the end of your career, what one accomplishment would you like people to remember you for?"

"What do you plan to be doing five years from today?"

MINITASK 6:
KNOW WHAT TO
LOOK AND LISTEN FOR

Listening, as we've noted, is the key to interviewing. Here are some of the things you want to listen for.

THREE IMPORTANT ANSWERS
YOU WANT TO HEAR

ANSWER 1:
"BOTH MY LONG-TERM WORK GOALS
AND LONG-TERM LIFE GOALS
ARE ORIENTED TOWARD THE JOB
YOU ARE OFFERING."

Of course the phrasing will undoubtedly be different. But you want to hear about the plans and hopes of the applicant. You don't want to hire a computer programmer who would rather be acting on the stage. You don't want to put an introvert in a salesperson's job. You don't want to stick an independent thinker on an assembly line any more than you want to put a rote worker in a group leader's job.

ANSWER 2:
"I'LL 'FIT IN' WITH THE JOB."
Again you aren't going to be satisfied simply to hear the applicant say these words. But if you listen carefully, you'll be able to hear whether or not the applicant can give this answer by his or her conduct. What you are really judging is maturity.

The last thing you want to do is hire a person who is too insecure to make a vital phone call to a hostile competitor or feels "out of place" at an important meeting. You don't want to hire someone who doesn't have the confidence to "chew out" a non-performing supplier or the assurance to comfort a customer who didn't receive an order on time. You also don't want to see the person you hire acting "silly" with his or her fellow employees, managers, or subordinates.

If the applicant's personal stature measures up to the

job, they will be comfortable in it. Their success will seem "natural."

ANSWER 3:
"I KNOW HOW TO PRODUCE RESULTS."

Again you have to listen "between the lines" to hear this answer. As mentioned earlier, in life there are the "doers" and the "wheel spinners," and employees are drawn from both camps. Since, ultimately, you are going to be concerned with results, you want to know that this person knows how to get them.

You don't want to see the person you hire always "appear" to be busy, but in reality never getting much done. You don't want to count on the new employee for a report that you need on June 7th only to learn on June 6th that it hasn't been started. You don't want excuses or explanations. You want results.

If the applicant is an achiever, his or her self-confidence will shine in the face of new challenges.

These, then, are the three answers that you want to hear—answers that will tell you that the applicant's goals are aligned with the job. Getting to them is usually just a matter of a few guiding questions and some intense listening. Remember, this is a positive test. You want to hear the right answers to get the right person.

Besides listening, there are many other items you will want to look for.

SELF-CONFIDENCE

Here is a quick test that a manager we know uses when hiring people to work in her restaurant. She is concerned that they have enough self-confidence to come across as pleasing even to disagreeable customers. She enters the interview and refuses to smile at the applicant.

It is the easiest thing for a person to *return* a smile, but if you don't smile first, it takes substantial self-confidence on the part of the other person to smile. This manager witholds her smile for just a bit at first. She sees how long it takes the other person to start smiling and become friendly. Then, of course, she returns the smile and opens up. But in the process, she's gotten a clue to the self-confidence of the applicant.

This technique is particularly useful for jobs involving customer service. Its drawback is that it tends to inhibit rapport.

NEATNESS

Observe the applicant's shoes, hair, and fingernails. Applicants know that the interview is important. If they are well groomed for it, it's a good sign. If they haven't cared enough to be neat for the interview, however, what does that say for their future commitment to the job?

TENSION

The interview is a stress situation. Look for how well applicants handle that stress. Do they drum their fingers, bite nails, or exhibit any other uncontrollable mannerism? If they can't handle the strain of the interview, how will they manage the day-to-day stress of the job?

RESPONSIBILITY

Note whether applicants are on time for their interviews. Do they blame others for past problems or accept responsibility themselves? (Watch out for blamers.) Do they bad-mouth former employers and associates? Blamers usually feel guilty for their own bad past performance.

INTERVIEWER WEAKNESSES TO WATCH FOR

In addition to applicants' strengths and weaknesses, there are a number of interviewer weaknesses you also should be aware of in yourself.

CONTRASTING APPLICANTS

If one applicant comes in and is weak in all areas, the next applicant, even if he or she is just average, may seem super by contrast. Try not to judge applicants against other applicants but against a set of criteria.

FIRST IMPRESSIONS

First impressions are important. They can also be wrong. The applicant who stumbles when shaking hands can give you the impression he or she is a bumbler. But that impression may be totally wrong. Be on guard not to be swayed by first impressions.

BAD IMPRESSIONS

An applicant may have one overriding characteristic that gives you such a bad impression you overlook everything else. Maybe the applicant has bad breath. You can't stand the breath and so you grade the applicant down on everything else. It also works the other way. If an applicant is physically attractive, you may grade up everything else. Watch out for the single impression that overrides other judgment. (These are sometimes called the "halo" and "horn" effects.) Each of us has our own biases. When interviewing it's important to try to recognize them and work at not letting them sway our judgment.

FORGETTING TO LISTEN

Many people tend to concentrate on the words being spoken. Don't forget to listen to the feelings behind the words. Listen to the person and not just to what he or she says.

Interviewing is more an art than a science. There are no perfect questions to ask, just as there are no perfect responses. Mostly, you are dealing with impressions and making judgments based on those.

If you follow the six minitasks outlined here, however, you should be able to conduct efficient interviews that in most cases will be highly revealing.

TASK 6

SETTING EMPLOYEE GOALS

*To cross the raging river,
find the stepping stones.*

Old Chinese proverb

About a decade ago a technique called "management by objective" became extremely popular and was heralded as the final answer to managing. Essentially this technique said that to manage successfully, what was needed was to establish verifiable objectives for each worker. The employee would work toward those objectives and when they were achieved, both the worker and the manager would recognize this fact through some sort of mutually agreed upon verification. Then they could move on to other tasks. Multiply this by all the workers and managers and an entire company could move forward toward achieving its goals.

Today management by objective is commonly used in many companies. In this chapter we're going to look at it again, point out what we feel are some of its weak points, and suggest ways to improve on them.

PROBLEMS WITH MANAGEMENT BY OBJECTIVE

While on paper management by objective looks good, in real life we have found that it almost always does *not* fully work for three reasons:

BOTH MANAGERS AND WORKERS ONLY GIVE IT LIP SERVICE

To most of us management by objective is like the I.D. badge worn at many larger organizations. The company says you must wear the badge, even though it looks ridiculous hanging onto a blouse or shirt. So you pin on the badge, satisfy the company and go on doing whatever you were doing before.

Management by objective is similar. The company says you must manage by objective. So at a set time the manager sits down with the employee(s) and they fill out the objective forms together. Then the forms are filed and everybody goes back to whatever they were doing before. No more real attention is paid to the management technique than is paid to the I.D. badge.

If at the end of the period the objective is achieved, the manager and worker(s) are congratulated, although the real credit is given to the management technique. If the objective wasn't achieved, then new objectives are set and the technique is credited with making clear that a problem existed. No matter what happens, the technique always comes off making the manager look like a winner.

THE OBJECTIVES ARE OFTEN UNREALISTIC

In companies where the managers alone are allowed to set the objectives, the workers often fail to achieve them simply because they are too difficult. The managers often write in their most optimistic work dreams without taking into account the workers' abilities and enthusiasm (or lack of it).

In companies where workers are allowed to set the objectives, usually little is accomplished because they are set too low. Workers are aware that promotions and bonuses hinge on successful performance, so they "stack the cards." They write in objectives they can easily attain, hoping to reap quick and easy rewards.

In companies where managers and workers sit down together, compromise is often the rule. Management's real goals may not be achieved, and workers still may feel that the objectives are too difficult.

MANAGERS USE
THE TECHNIQUE TO
STOP MANAGING

The real pitfall of management by objective for managers, however, is that it allows them to never again have to take the blame. If a supervisor wants to know how things are going, the managers can always pull out those objective sheets to demonstrate that they are on top of the job. If company objectives aren't met, it is always possible for them to say that company objectives were unrealistic.

Discussions always revolve around objectives (and sometimes their verifiability). No longer is the subject the managers, or their ability to manage. Rather it is the technique that is the subject. Thus managers can use the technique of "management by objective" to get out of doing real managing.

WHY MANAGEMENT BY
OBJECTIVE CAN FAIL

In our opinion the real shortcoming of "management by objective" is that the technique itself is essentially flawed. The flaw is that "management by objective" is external and artificial. In some parlance it might be called a "no brainer." It doesn't actively engage the manager in the vital task of managing, but rather puts management "on paper." The essence of "management by objective" is in following a procedure. If you follow the procedure, you can't lose. Thinking and vital interacting aren't always necessary.

At its most basic level, however, management is dealing with people. And people are not sheets of paper.

No matter what we write down on our objective sheets, performance will hinge on individual effort. If we don't see to it that the effort is forthcoming, the worker—and the manager—will fail.

To put it another way, regardless of what "management by objective" hopes to achieve, managing simply isn't mechanical. It's organic and interactive. It isn't something like a machine that you set up once, and leave alone, not coming back until it's finished. Managing is nurturing people.

MANAGEMENT THROUGH ACHIEVEMENT

To correct the deficiencies of "management by objective," we suggest a strategy we have named "management through achievement." An example will help illustrate how it works.

THE PITCHING GAME

We developed the following game for training new teachers to create situations that will help them become successful teachers. It is based on the familiar game of pitching pennies.

In the pitching game, second graders are asked to pitch little colored disks (about the size and weight of pennies) into a small-necked basket. The children are placed on the "pitching line" and the basket can be placed a marked distance away from them anywhere from two to seven feet. To illustrate the game to new teachers, at least three second graders are required, each playing the game for the first time, and each unaware of how others have played it before.

The first student that comes in is given five disks and told that the goal of the game is to get three of the five disks into the basket. The basket is placed seven feet away. Typically the child will move to the pitching line and begin pitching disks. Because the basket is relatively small, it is almost impossible to get even one disk in at seven feet, let alone three. After a few sets of five, the student will usually get discouraged and stop playing the game.

Now another student is brought in. This student is told that the goal is to get the disks into the basket. But this time the child is told he or she may place the basket wherever desired, but as far away from the pitching line as possible. Typically this student will start by placing the basket about half-way, perhaps three or four feet. At this distance, it's still hard to get the disks in, so the student will move the basket closer, to perhaps two feet. There, the game is easy. As soon as the student succeeds at two feet, he or she moves it to three. When there's some success at three, it is moved to four. Typically students will move the basket to four or sometimes five feet before deciding it's too difficult and quit the game.

Finally the last student is brought in. The basket is placed on the two foot mark by the teacher and the student is told the goal is to get three out of five disks in. This is normally achieved on the first or second try. At this point the student is praised and the teacher moves the basket to three feet. Again the student is told the goal is to get three out of five disks in it. Upon success there is more praise and the teacher moves the basket to four feet and then to five. At five feet, it is pretty hard, but typically the students are able to succeed rapidly, drawing on the experience they gained at closer levels.

Now it's moved to six feet out where it's really tough. As long as the student shows enthusiasm, the basket is left at six. However, as the student begins to get frustrated the basket is brought back to five or even four feet, where a few successful tosses restore confidence. Then it's moved back to six. Almost invariably the student soon achieves three out of five disks in at six feet. Now the basket is moved to seven feet out, where getting it in is next to impossible for a second grader. But by now the student is very confident in his or her ability and in many cases, the seven-foot level is achieved without a great deal more difficulty than the six-foot level.

BEHIND THE GAME

New teachers are asked to notice what happened in this game. When the child was told the goal was seven feet, nearly all students simply stood at the pitching line and tried to throw the disks in. But because they didn't have the experience and confidence of achieving success at shorter distances, they quickly failed. When the child was allowed to set his or her own distance for success, invariably he or she selected a distance far less than the maximum attainable.

Only when the student was guided from a small achievement to ever greater achievements was he or she eventually successful in getting the disks into the basket at the maximum distance.

This game shows prospective teachers that the key to building successful students is providing opportunities for them to first achieve and gain confidence in small ways. Simply expecting top performance right off the bat won't work. Expecting them to do it on their own won't work. Only through a series of carefully guided situations where achievement is built on achievement can success be finally grasped.

Of course there are exceptions. Some students simply don't have the dexterity in the second grade to get the disks in the basket even when it is only three or four feet away. They simply shouldn't have been selected for this exercise.

A very few others are smart and self-motivated. When faced with the basket seven feet away, they quickly realize that the key is gaining experience in tossing. On their own, without being coached, they move the basket closer until they achieve some success, then they move it farther and farther away until they are able to achieve seven feet. In a business setting such people would be known as self-motivating or as "sparkplugs."

The vast majority of students, however, are somewhere in between the ones who can't do the task at all and the ones who are sufficiently smart and motivated to figure out how to do it on their own. It's to this vast majority that teachers learn to address themselves for most of their efforts.

For managers, the situation is not much different. To build successful employees, you need to provide an environment where your employees can build on ever-increasing achievements until their long-range goals, difficult though they may seem, become attainable.

That's why we call our strategy "management through achievement." It's not simply a matter of setting goals or objectives. It's managing people so that they achieve many small goals on the way to larger ones. *It is in the creation of an environment where workers can achieve that the real management of people takes place.*

A STRATEGIC PLAN
FOR MANAGEMENT
BY ACHIEVEMENT

There are five steps to setting achievable goals for workers. As managers you need to act on all five:

NEEDS ASSESSMENT

This can be as simple as your supervisor telling you, "This is what we need."

Or it can be more complex. It can be you as manager, your workers, and your supervisor all getting together and coming to a mutual decision on what's needed. Or it can be something that you are expected to decide all on your own. How needs assessment is carried out really depends on the type of company.

What needs assessment comes down to, however, is that it determines your own work goals.

WORKER OBJECTIVES

Once you know what your own goals are, you must determine objectives for your employees that will help you to realize these goals. In other words, you must figure out what tasks you want your employees to do that will result in your achieving your work goals. This is similar to the technique used in the standard "management by objectives" plan.

WORKER ASSESSMENT

This is a vital step. From your knowledge of your employees' abilities, you must now make judgments regarding their chances of attaining the goals you've set up. In other words, you must match the person to the job. If an employee is a "sparkplug," perhaps you can simply explain the ultimate goal you have for them and if they concur, let them figure out how to achieve it on their own. Note: it's a very rare employee with whom you can do this.

Like the second graders who lack dexterity, some of your workers may never be able to achieve certain objectives. You must not assign tasks which aren't achievable or frustration will result for all. In these cases, you must try to move such workers to tasks more suited to them.

In most cases, however, the worker can achieve success if properly motivated. That is, if he or she brings enthusiasm and energy to the job, the objective can be reached. Your goal is to bring these qualities out in the employees.

SETTING ACHIEVABLE GOALS

This doesn't take long to do, but it can be the one task which requires your greatest concentration. You need to cut up the pie which is your ultimate objective. You need to cut it into easily swallowed slices. Each slice then becomes a separate goal attainable by the employee.

You need to figure out the *steps* which will lead to your final goal. That way the employee can achieve each step along the way until your final objective is met.

Note: Borrowing from the techniques of "management by objective," you need to be sure that each goal is verifiable in a way that will be convincing both to you and to the worker.

FOLLOWING THROUGH

Once you've set your objectives, the amount of time required to manage should be quite small. You meet with the employee and explain your short-range goal, explain its importance, and gain the acceptance and concurrence of the employee.

If the goal is really achievable there should be a fair amount of enthusiasm on the part of the employee. On the other hand if the short-term goal is too difficult the worker will probably be resistant. You should be on the look-out for this resistance as it indicates an error in *your* planning. Now is the time to ask the worker for input and to *listen* to what is said. Now is the time to restructure the short-term goal until it is more realistic, more suited to the worker's ability.

Once the employee understands and concurs with the *achievable* short-term goal, you simply follow through. Keep a eye on what's happening to be sure the goal is achievable. Encouragement helps here. You should stay alert so that as soon as the employee achieves the short-term goal, you step in with praise. Then immediately go through the discussion process again with the next short-term goal, the next *step* in the process along the way to the longer-term goal. Remember to encourage and then praise for achievement.

In this way you manage your workers so that they move from achievement to achievement until they get to the ultimate objective. Ever-increasing achievements have built success for them and for you.

DEALING WITH PROBLEMS

Problems can occur along the way. You may notice that the worker has slowed down, isn't making progress, appears *lazy*. It's time to reassess. Was the goal unrealistic? Are the worker's abilities and knowledge less than you originally thought? Is there an external problem facing the worker?

If the goal wasn't realistic, perhaps it should be broken down further into more easily achieved steps that are more in accordance with the worker's abilities and knowledge. In such a case after a period of frustration, it is vital that the worker *quickly* get an achievement so that he or she has the confidence to move on. Therefore this redesigned goal should be readily achievable.

If there's an external problem, refer the worker to appropriate counseling. A manager should never try to be a therapist.

AN ACHIEVABLE
GOAL EXAMPLE

Fred was a plant manager. He oversaw nine other managers at a facility which produced bathroom fixtures which were sold nationwide. Fred's sub-managers handled every level of production at the plant from the purchase of raw materials, through fabrication, into plating, and finally into packaging.

Fred's goals were set in large part by the sales people. He had to keep production up to sales. (Occasionally he would have to cut production back to match lowered sales.)

Fred followed the "Management Through Achievement" plan.

1. First he would very clearly define his production goals for a specific period.

2. Next he would determine exactly what was needed from each area of production from the purchase of raw materials through packaging in order to achieve those goals.

3. Next he would judge which of his workers (sub-managers) were best suited to achieving his goals. Sometimes this meant switching workers from one area of the plant to another. Sometimes it meant hiring a new employee and also transferring or laying off an old one.

4. Next he would break down the goals for each separate sub-manager into small parts. In some cases, monthly assembly line goals would be broken down into weekly or even hourly goals. The first goal might be 17 units an hour. When that was achieved, the next goal would be 18 units an hour. The ultimate goal might be 25 an hour.

In another case reduced breakage might be the goal. Breakage would be first reduced from the current 7 percent to 6.5 percent through specific safety and quality control procedures. Then the goal would be set at 6 percent, and so forth.

In yet other cases, his sub-managers' goals would be increased enthusiasm and creativity from their workers, evidenced by less absenteeism, fewer accidents, and greater productivity. Here specific morale-building techniques were to be introduced and evaluated one at a time.

5. Finally he followed through. He sat down with each sub-manager and explained the immediate short-term goal. Fred worked hard to get his employees to agree with the goals. He knew the key to his success was working together. Where a manager saw that the goal could be achieved, that person usually concurred and was enthusiastic. Fred let the manager get started.

Where the manager complained, Fred asked questions, reevaluated, and usually came up with an easier goal. Where the manager wasn't engaged and didn't seem to care, Fred again asked questions, reevaluated, and came up with a more challenging short-term goal.

As work progressed, Fred watched. He adjusted goals where necessary, gave encouragement, and praised achievement. As short-term goals were achieved, new, mutually acceptable ones were set. In this manner Fred eventually was able to achieve his own goals set for him by the sales force.

PUTTING THE
STRATEGY TO WORK

The goal-setting strategy outlined in this chapter is based on people, not paper. It requires *active* management.

It means that you have to be aware of what's going on. On a regular basis (daily, weekly, monthly, or whatever is appropriate) you must check up so you know where the workers are on the road to achieving their goals. You must be alert for signs of "lazy" behavior which signals a problem with achievement, and you must take appropriate corrective steps.

Encouragement is required, as is praise.

What you should quickly discover, however, is how much extra time you have. Put this strategy into operation and you will suddenly find you are doing pure management. No longer are you doing your workers' jobs for them or having to constantly oversee them. Pure managing means fine tuning a smooth-running operation.

Remember, it's not how much time you spend, or how many reams of papers you fill writing down objectives, that makes the difference. Rather it's knowing that employees wish to succeed and will work hard if they can see a way to achieve.

TASK 7

ENCOURAGING (STROKING I)

I'm confident you can do the job.

Manager to new worker

E ncouraging, or stroking, as it is sometimes called, is a necessary follow-up once goals are established. Encouraging shows workers that you are alert and that you care. Note however, that encouraging without first having established goals often backfires; workers may feel it is insincere.

WHAT IS ENCOURAGING?

"Encouraging" means stimulating people, giving them hope in their own progress, letting them know that they are on the right track. We have said that achieving is a natural desire and that it is the best motivator. People will work especially hard when they know they can achieve.

On any job, however, there are bound to be fairly long periods between achievements. Encouragement fills this gap. It is a kind of support that tells people that while they may not have yet achieved their goal, they are getting closer all the time.

WHY ENCOURAGE?

For most people it is far easier to give up than to continue with a hard task. This is particularly true where there is no real evidence of progress. This frequently occurs when a new employee comes into a company and every face he or she sees is a stranger. All the procedures are unknown. The work station is unfamiliar. It can be overwhelming and the person can get discouraged rather quickly.

Even an old employee starting toward a new goal can experience dismay at seeing the enormous size of the task to be accomplished. Such a person may say, "It can't be done," and give up before trying.

Both the new and the old employee may have achievable goals that they are working toward. However, particularly at the beginning, getting started can be the hardest step. A good manager will offer encouragement.

We all want approval, and encouragement is a kind of unconditional approval. It lets employees know that they are personally all right, that they are doing the right thing. As sentimental as it may sound, in a very real sense encouragement is the company's way of giving love, trust, and acceptance.

WHEN TO ENCOURAGE

Proper encouragement of new employees, particularly during the first few days, can influence their attitudes toward work for years to come. A man we know tells the following story to illustrate this point.

"As a college student, I took a part-time job with the local office of a nationwide credit investigating company—a huge company with over 10,000 employees. I was hired as an investigator and paid a very small amount for work accomplished.

"To this day, more than twenty years later, I remember how all the office managers went out of their way to introduce themselves during my first two or three days, to ask if I needed anything, and just to say how happy they were to have me there and how sure they were that I would work out fine. At least three times in my first week there, the general manager, who oversaw nearly seventy people, came over to offer encouragement.

"Needless to say, all this attention really pepped me up, and I know I made an extra effort to do good work because of it."

Encouraging a new employee starts the person off on the right foot and keeps them on the right track. It is particularly useful, as noted, during the first two or three days.

Another time to encourage is any time a worker starts a new task. Phrases such as, "I'm sure you can do it," or "You're a real asset to the company," or "We really appreciate what you've done for us in the past and we're glad you're the person handling this project," can be helpful. The actual words don't count nearly as much as does the positive tone.

Encouragement can also be used as a stimulant when you see a worker slowing down (appearing "lazy"). Phrases such as "How are you coming along? Is there anything I can do to help?" or "I really like what you've done thus far and can hardly wait to see the rest," can be effective.

In addition to knowing when to encourage, it is also useful to know that encouragement works when specific types of behavior occur. You can be fairly sure encouragement will help when a worker exhibits:

1. Slowness
2. Fear (at tackling a new task)
3. Insecurity (about acceptance either from the company, management, or other workers)
4. Weakness (doesn't currently have the ability or knowledge to complete the task, but can learn)
5. Depression (providing it doesn't have other causes)

Notice that in each of these cases the natural tendency might be to criticize, berate, or even "chew out" the employee for the behavior. But you must understand the cause behind the behavior is a lack of motivation resulting from insufficient achievement. Criticism of such behavior, therefore, is inappropriate. Encouragement— giving unconditional acceptance, saying it's all right and that you believe in the person—is the correct antidote.

Sometimes the worker only needs to talk it out. *Listening* and simply nodding approval as an employee explains a problem or frustration can be an extremely effective means of encouraging.

ENCOURAGING MUST *ALWAYS* BE POSITIVE

Remember that encouragement is a small reward, a kind of stroking. It must be freely given and it must make the receiver feel better about himself or herself. (Sometimes patting the person on the back or touching their arm while you're speaking to them helps get across the idea that you really do care.)

To summarize, there are three times when you want to encourage:

1. When a person is new on the job.
2. When someone is starting a new task.
3. When a worker slows down (appears "lazy").

OVERKILL

Many people believe that if one pill works, a whole bottle will work a lot better. With encouragement, that's not the case. Encouragement has to be administered sparingly. It's a balm that must be hoarded to be applied only when there's a real need.

A great danger with encouraging is to go around doing it all the time. It's wonderful to be positive because it results in so much positive feedback for yourself. However, for the people on the receiving end, indiscriminate encouragement soon loses its value.

If you encourage every day, or even several times a day, people may begin wondering just what is the value of that encouragement? They may think that perhaps you're the sort of person who just wanders around with encouraging things constantly babbling from your lips. Hence the value of your encouraging is diminished, and when you really need it, it won't have the potency it should have.

Even worse can happen. If you encourage too much, employees may feel that you are insincere. They may begin to believe that you really don't care about them, aren't really trying to help them, but are simply engaged in a management trick, a kind of manipulation. The result can be a loss of trust which can disable your ability to manage. *Trust once lost can be very difficult to regain.*

DIFFERENCE BETWEEN ENCOURAGEMENT AND CRITICISM

In a later chapter we'll explore how to give criticism, but for now it's important to understand the difference between encouragement and criticism. Encouragement is *unconditional* acceptance of the worker. Criticism is *conditional* acceptance.

When you encourage, you say something like "I approve of you and your work." On the other hand, when you criticize, you might say "I'll approve of your work if you improve this one area." In criticism, approval hinges on a change of behavior on the part of the employee. In encouragement, approval is unconditional.

Be sure you understand the difference and that you aren't inadvertantly criticizing when you mean to encourage.

PEOPLE WHO ARE DIFFICULT TO ENCOURAGE

Some people are difficult to encourage. The classic example here is the egocentric person, the "know-it-all."

You walk up to this person and say, "I think you're doing a good job there." He or she turns to you and replies, "Of course I am. Why would you expect anything different?"

The natural tendency is to say to yourself "Well, pardon me for caring," and storm away without giving any more encouragement.

Another version of this sort of person is the one who replies, "Don't bug me, man," to your encouragement. This is the hostile worker, the one who by his or her words or tone warns you not to get close.

What is operating in both these cases is a kind of defense mechanism. Assuming there isn't a severe underlying psychological problem (which there might be and which you should not attempt to handle—remember, managers are not therapists), the worker is probably burdened by unexpressed fear or at least lack of confidence. However, instead of being open about the fear or lack of confidence, this worker turns the emotion into a kind of shield. Aloof or angry workers may actually be denying their own feelings.

When you offer encouragement, these workers may

believe that you think they're having problems. But since they won't admit, even to themselves, that they might indeed be having problems, they deny the need for encouragement. In fact, they resent it.

How do you handle this? Sometimes you simply can't. This type of person may just not allow you to encourage. In such cases, you may need to wait until there is some actual achievement and then praise. (See the next chapter.) In some cases, however, you can encourage once you gain the trust of the individual. One way to do this is to reverse the situation. Instead of encouraging them, ask them to help you. One manager we know handles this difficult situation by first identifying something the worker has recently done successfully. Then she says something like "By the way, I'm having trouble with this. Can you help me?"

The worker now gives the manager aid for which the manager can then appropriately express thanks and even throw in a few words of approval. In this way the worker gets a small reward and feels good about his or her abilities or knowledge. In other words, the difficult worker learns to accept encouragement.

Encouragement is one of the best tools a manager has. It doesn't take long to do and when used appropriately can yield enormous results, not the least of which is that it even makes the person giving it feel better!

TASK 8

PRAISING
(STROKING II)

*The sweetest of all sounds
is praise.*

Xenophon

*Many know how to flatter,
Few know how to praise.*

Wendell Phillips

Praising is a vital part of managing. Giving praise (another form of stroking) is acknowledging the achievement of a specific goal or a desired behavior. It lets workers know that you recognize their work. Your recognition puts a stamp of approval on their achievement.

Praising should not be underated. It motivates employees to keep achieving. Some managers feel that if you don't praise good work, you'll have to make up for it in some other way, such as giving bonuses or salary increases. Praising, however, can't be indiscriminate. There are established rules which must be followed.

RULES FOR PRAISING

GIVE PRAISE ONLY FOR THE ACHIEVEMENT OF A SPECIFIC GOAL

You have to be careful. If you go to Judy to praise without first checking to see that there's been achievement, you set yourself up to lose. Suppose you casually remark as you pass by, "Say, that's really good work."

Judy may turn and ask, "What is?"

In other words, she didn't know she had achieved anything. Was there something she missed that deserved praise? Why how wonderful, she may be thinking. Now tell me what it is that I've done so I can feel good about it, too.

Since you weren't watching carefully, you now scramble, looking for something to praise. "Why, I just meant your, well, your regular work."

"But I just broke this item I'm trying to assemble."

"Well, of course, I mean your day-to-day work, not necessarily your work of the moment," you say, feeling rather embarrassed.

Judy now feels let down. She hadn't really done anything praiseworthy. What's worse, she now may feel that though you are well-intentioned, you aren't alert. She had thought you were a careful manager aware of what she is doing. Now you've let her know that you aren't as watchful as she thought. In the future maybe she'll let a few things slip.

Praise is recognition of good work. The good work must be there for the praise to be justified. That means that you must take the time to be aware of just where people are on the road to achieving their objectives, so that on the day the objective is achieved, you are there with your praise. A super manager keeps a sufficiently careful watch, knows when small goals are achieved on the road to bigger ones, and is able to give praise along the way.

When praise is appropriate, it tells workers that you are alert to their progress and appreciate it. This makes them feel important, needed, and worthwhile. It builds their self-esteem, and that is what will carry them forward to greater achievements.

PRAISE MUST BE APPROPRIATE FOR THE ACHIEVEMENT

INSINCERE PRAISE

If Jim completes the sale of a small insurance policy, his manager wants to praise him for his efforts. However, if the manager says "Wow, that's terrific. That's the best sale in the world! You're a dynamite salesperson! I bet you feel proud! Wowee, you're the greatest in sales! I don't know what the company would do without you," Jim, of course, is bound to be suspicious. He just sold a $1,500 term policy with a $70 premium. If this is how his manager reacts, then the manager must be:

1. Insincere
2. Desperate for business (so why is Jim working there?)
3. Manipulative (trying to praise Jim because he wants some hidden thing in return.)

Jim may have been feeling modestly proud of his small achievement. Now, he may feel embarrassed by it. Instead of making him feel good, feel successful, his manager may have made him feel suspicious and used.

INSUFFICIENT PRAISE

There is, of course, the other extreme—giving insufficient praise for a major accomplishment. Jim sells a group life insurance policy to a company with 130 employees. The first year's premium is $30,000. He comes back beaming.

His manager glances at the policy, mumbles "Good work, keep it up," and goes on with whatever he had been doing.

He's taken the wind out of Jim's sails. This was an outstanding sale, perhaps a once-in-a-year occurrence for him. He's thrilled by it. He sees it as a real achievement, as the attainment of a significant sales goal, as a measure of his success.

His manager has just shown him how wrong he is. The faint praise suggests that it was just a normal sort of sale, the kind that's to be expected of him, no big deal.

Jim is likely to either become frustrated, feel defeated, and slow down *or* to go to someone else (possibly a competitor), tell that person what he's done, and there get the kind of praise he feels he deserves.

Remember, when workers achieve they not only feel they deserve praise, they demand that the praise be appropriate to the achievement.

PRAISE MUST BE APPROPRIATE
TO THE PERSON

Some people deserve praise, want praise, but don't know
how to handle it. Imagine taking a shy person to a restaurant on their birthday. At the end of dinner, by ar-
rangement, out come all the waiters and waitresses carrying a cake and singing "Happy Birthday." An extrovert
might shine on such an occasion. But a shy person may
feel humiliated. It's not that a celebration wasn't called
for. The point is that the celebration should be geared
to the individual's temperament.

Alice is an extrovert. She's totally open, constantly
talking with her co-workers. She's just attained an important goal. You go out and praise her achievement in
front of her co-workers. Alice beams in delight.

Alicia is an introvert. She is quiet, seldom speaks
unless first spoken to. She, too, has just attained an important goal. You ask her into your office or take her
aside and quietly tell her how pleased you are with what
she's accomplished. Alicia also beams in quiet delight
while looking around to be sure no one has overheard.

You've matched your praise to the individual. But
reverse the situations—praise Alice in private, Alicia in
front of her co-workers—and see the damage you could
do.

THE DIFFERENCE BETWEEN
PRAISE AND ENCOURAGEMENT

As we said in the last chapter, encouragement is the unconditional approval of a person's work. Encouragement isn't earned, it is given gratuitously. It shows that
you want people to succeed, that you have the confi-

dence that they will succeed. It gives them the courage to move forward through what might be a difficult task.

Praise, on the other hand, is approval of an achievement. It is *always earned*. Never give praise gratuitously. Never praise someone who hasn't achieved something. Praise shows recognition. It lets people know that you are alert to their achievements. It lets them know that the company appreciates what they've done. It's the reward that makes all the work possible.

PRAISE AS THE SUCCESSFUL COMPLETION OF A TASK

Praise is also the signal that terminates the progress to a completed goal. The worker does the work, then brings it to you. By praising, you let them know that you and the company approve and agree that the objective was achieved. This allows the person to put that old goal past them and start toward a new one.

Praise, like a smile, is free. It costs nothing to give, yet can bring enormous returns. We have never met a successful manager who didn't know how to praise. We also have never met a successful manager who didn't follow the three rules of praising.

TASK 9

CRITICIZING

*There is no room for
negativism in the workplace.*

Engraved on a CEO's desk

I t's very important that managers understand what criticism should not be before attempting to use it. Criticism should *not* be:

☐ Bawling out another person
☐ Being critical of another person
☐ Reprimanding for bad performance
☐ Being negative

This may seem surprising since the word "criticize" has such negative connotations in our language. To most people, it implies something quite bad. Many assume, in fact, that to criticize means to be negative in dealing with others. This is unfortunate, because such "bad criticism" is almost always counter-productive.

An employee is often worse after negative criticism than before. A manager may intend to improve a worker, but after bad criticism, is chagrined to see that the work performance or behavior actually slips. Some managers, having seen this undesired result of bad criticism, have even begun to think that there is no real place for criticism in managing people.

Nothing could be further from the truth. Criticism is a way of correcting the behavior or work performance of an employee. But to be effective, it must be handled properly. Criticism is like a stick of dynamite. It has the potential for either great good or great harm.

Working with criticism, like working with dynamite, takes care and understanding. It is important to understand the difference between negative and positive criticism and know how to give constructive criticism. It is also important not to have unrealistic hopes for what criticism may accomplish. It can indeed make significant changes, but it isn't a miracle cure.

THE GOAL OF CRITICISM

The goal of criticism is almost always to improve behavior or work performance or both. There is normally a positive objective.

Thus we usually end up criticizing employees or workers who aren't doing what they are supposed to. Henry isn't producing his quota of sales, so we criticize (we try to get him to increase production). Phyllis isn't assembling enough product and we criticize her (we want her to assemble faster). Sally isn't spending enough time at her work, so we criticize (we want her at her work station, not at the water cooler). In other words, our goal in criticizing is to get the worker to either improve work performance or behavior (or both).

PROBLEMS WITH CRITICISM

Problems usually arise, however, when you lose sight of your goal for the criticism because of your own personal feelings. Your supervisor may have just pointed out that your production is down. How can that be, you wonder, until you look around and see Sally chatting with a friend by the water cooler. That's the reason! You storm over and criticize (chew out) Sally.

Your goal was to get Sally to stop taking so many breaks. The result, however, is that you probably only antagonized her, so that in the future she'll be tempted to do the opposite of what you want.

Sometimes criticism isn't angry, but just awkward. Henry's sales are slipping. You quickly see that the problem is that he isn't spending enough time "cold calling" (making blind phone calls to potential clients).

You aren't angry, you just want to help. So you go up to Henry and say, "Your problem is you're not reaching out to the clients." Henry looks at us, retorts, "I don't have a problem, you do!" and takes the rest of the day off.

Your friendly criticism was taken the wrong way and produced quite an unexpected and opposite result. Thus even when you're not angry, your criticism may turn out to be negative and work against you.

NEGATIVE CRITICISM

If ever a management technique required a clear strategy, it's criticizing. In no other area are you as likely to accomplish the opposite of what you want. Wrong or negative criticism is often simply the "natural" thing to do. You may just be inexperienced in knowing how to give constructive criticism. Sometimes good criticism just never gets said.

Therefore, let's take a moment to look at what negative or wrong criticism really is. We've already suggested it can be counterproductive. Now let's see why that happens. To do this, we'll take an example from the world of animals.

NEGATIVE CRITICISM
IN TRAINING ANIMALS

From television or visits to aquatic parks and circuses, you're probably somewhat familiar with techniques used by animal trainers. These techniques mainly involve positive reinforcement for good behavior without undue criticism of bad. For example, the killer whale performs the trick and is given a fish as reward. If the killer whale fails to perform, the trainer scolds modestly, encourages, and then urges the whale to try again. It tries, performs, and then gets its reward.

A dog is supposed to jump through a hoop. It tries and fails. The trainer comforts the dog, then carefully leads it through the hoop by hand, finally urging it to try again. The dog tries and this time succeeds and is immediately rewarded with a treat.

Notice that there is little negative criticism in these examples. The technique is positive. When the whale doesn't perform, the trainer might say a word of scolding to acknowledge that he or she has seen the bad performance, but immediately the animal is encouraged to try again. When the dog doesn't perform, the trainer shows it exactly what's required and then urges it to try again.

Both cases are a form of criticism. Neither the whale nor the dog get their rewards when they don't perform. They may even be mildly scolded. But at no time is either the whale or the dog made to feel that they are bad animals. There is no attack by the trainer on the animal itself. The trainer always keeps in the forefront of his or her mind the goal, namely that the animal should perform the trick.

We have been told by trainers that if someone who is trying to teach an animal a trick severely scolds it or even hits it, the animal is likely to become so defensive that it will be unable to perform the trick again that day. Repeated negative criticism over even a short period of time can prevent the animal from being able to perform for a much longer period.

In other words, negative criticism causes the animal to lose confidence in both the trainer and in its own abilities. This in turn results in an inability to perform the desired goal.

NEGATIVE CRITICISM IN CHANGING PEOPLE'S BEHAVIOR

But what about people? We are certainly far more sophisticated than whales or dogs.

Yes we are, but like animals, we react adversely to negative criticism of any kind. Consider your own behavior. If you've just completed a difficult task and someone comes up to you and says, "Finally done, huh? Boy are you slow. You should be able to go twice as fast," are you likely to receive that person's criticism warmly and act postively on it?

On the other hand, suppose the same person says, "Congratulations on finishing. You did a good job. For your next challenge I'd like you to try to increase your speed a bit." Are you more likely to strive harder now?

PERSONALIZING NEGATIVE CRITICISM

People, like animals, tend to take negative criticism to heart. It really doesn't matter if someone is only criticizing their work. If it's negative, they *always* assume the comments are about themselves.

A manager moves up to a worker and says, "Say Lew, your work looks terrible." Lew turns to a fellow worker and says, "Did you hear that? He said I look terrible." Lew "heard" the negative remark as a criticism of himself rather than his work.

A manager says to Jill, "Say, have you got a sloppy desk!" Later at lunch that day Jill says to a friend, "Can you imagine the nerve of that manager calling me a slob!"

Again, although the criticism was work-directed, the

worker took the negativism personally and "heard" the remark as a personal criticism. Of course, implicit in both remarks was the manager's goal to criticize bad work or behavior and thereby get the worker to improve or clean up her desk. But that's not the message that got across.

When you're negative, the *only* thing that gets across is the negativism. Specific work or behavior comments are brushed aside by the listener. Only the negativism comes across and that comes across personally.

Try this little test. Read the next paragraph and then, before moving on, try to determine exactly what the manager wants:

As Peter puts down the phone, the manager walked up and said, "Caught you spinning your wheels!" It's people like you who are keeping this company in the red. This makes me so mad, I'm docking you for that call. There's a pay phone outside . . . use it!"

What's happening here? What is the manager's goal? What has he accomplished?

Peter's reaction is anger. "He accused me of being a wheel spinner. He think's there's something wrong with me. Where does he get off judging me?"

As it turns out, Peter had just made a phone call to his girlfriend to ask her out to dinner that night. However, the company had a firm policy against personal calls.

The manager was understandably upset. Peter was on the phone ostensibly doing business, while actually making a date. The manager's goal was to get Peter to stop making such calls. However, what got across was the manager's anger and his negative comments. As a result, Peter never got the message that the problem was his personal phone calls. Rather the message was that the manager had personally insulted him. In the future

Peter might either make personal phone calls as a matter of defiance (or disguise them more cleverly).

THE POWER OF
NEGATIVE CRITICISM

Because negative criticism tends to be taken personally, even if it's directed at work performance, it is extremely powerful. A tiny, tiny bit of negative criticism can totally devastate a person.

An example of this was noted in the late 1960s at San Francisco State College (now California State University of San Francisco) in the grading of English papers of students who had failed English proficiency tests.

Traditionally the grading was done by teaching assistants. They would mark the papers in red ink, indicating areas that were wrong as well as areas that needed improvement. The idea was that this written criticism was intended to improve the writing of the students.

However, when the student writers were given back their papers, allowed to read them, and then immediately asked what the criticism said, few could remember anything that had been written in the red ink except the impression it gave them that they personally were poor writers. *This was true even in cases where the criticism had been entirely complimentary!*

As an experiment the teaching assistants were instructed to now write in blue ink. Again as soon as the students had read their papers they were asked what was said. Now the majority clearly remembered the criticism, even if it had been negative.

The color of the ink determined how responsive the students were! There was nothing magical about blue ink.

What had happened was that over the years of attending school, students had learned to associate red ink with negative comments. When the students got back a paper with red scribbling on it, they immediately assumed it was negative criticism that would make them feel bad. As a result they just turned it off. They turned it off so acutely, in fact, that they couldn't even comprehend what had been written, even if it was positive.

The whole point, of course, is that even the smallest indication of negative criticism is taken personally and puts a person into a defensive reaction that obscures the content of what's being said.

If this is the case with written work, it is even more so with oral criticism. Toastmasters International, an excellent organization dedicated to helping people overcome the fear of speaking in public, has an evaluation period as part of each member club's regular meeting. Members give speeches and then during this "evaluation" period, other members critique how well the speakers did. However, it's an unwritten rule that no matter how bad the speaker was, the evaluator will always begin the evaluation commenting on some of the positive things the speaker did, and throughout the evaluation continue to occasionally make positive comments.

The point is that it's vitally important that the speaker hear positive things about his or her performance. This confirms in the speaker's mind that the evaluation is not a personal attack and that, on the whole, the speaker is a worthwhile person who, through a bit of work, can improve performance or behavior.

We've seen first-hand how disastrous results can occur when this policy is not followed. At one meeting we attended, a fairly good speaker gave a mediocre talk.

During evaluation, the evaluator immediately began criticizing everything from the speaker's use of voice modulation and hand movements to his topic organization. We agreed with all of the evaluator's comments, though not his method of presenting them.

Afterward the speaker was asked what he thought of the evaluation. We still remember his words. He said, "He told me that I'll never be able to give public talks. This is my last meeting. I quit!"

The speaker hadn't "heard" one word of the evaluator's criticism. The comments, all relatively minor, had been obscured by the method of presenting them. All that the speaker got out of it was the feeling that he, personally, was bad. Instead of helping, the evaluator had made the speaker feel diminished. He had, in fact, almost destroyed this person's self-confidence in terms of public speaking. It took much sympathetic and careful encouragement to get the speaker to stay with the club and to continue to improve his public speaking.

NO NEGATIVE CRITICISM

A little negative criticism goes a very long way. It goes so far, in fact, that our goal in this section is to convince you never to use it. So much more can be accomplished with positive criticism, and the dangers of producing an undesired reaction are so strong, that the rule to follow is simple:

Never give negative criticism.

In fact, a good way to remember it is to convince yourself that there is only positive criticism. If it's not positive, then it's something else. If you just keep in mind that when you are negative, you are not in any way achieving your goal of improving worker performance or behavior, then you're halfway home to being a good critic.

AVERSION THERAPY

Before leaving negative criticism, a word must be said about a kind of negative criticism that has become popular in recent years called "aversion therapy." Here a person is subjected to intense negative feelings about something in order to convince them to avoid it. For example, a smoker may purposely be made sick from inhaling smoke. The idea is that every time in the future that the person thinks of smoking, he or she will remember being sick and be averted from smoking.

Aversion therapy may have its place in a controlled environment when administered by people specially trained in its use and for a defined and specific problem (such as conquering the smoking habit or quitting alcohol addiction). But it has no place in the manager's bag of management techniques.

A manager who tries to extrapolate aversion therapy from the medical setting to the workplace is asking for nothing but trouble. The results may be poor performance, worsened behavior, and probably loss of personnel (not to mention possible legal consequences from angered employees).

Remember, a manager should never be a therapist.

POSITIVE CRITICISM

As we've said before, there is a natural desire to succeed. We all love success, in fact we thrive on it. Positive, or good, criticism makes use of this desire. Positive criticism expands a worker's horizon and shows the road to achievement.

WORKING WITH
RATHER THAN AGAINST

The essence of positive criticism is that it engages the worker's cooperation in improving and then shows how the improvement can be accomplished. In other words, with good criticism you are on the worker's side. You want someone to succeed and you help them so they can succeed.

An example is this illustration of a good teacher. Jill is having trouble with her math. She just can't do long division, and has just turned in a paper on which every answer was wrong. Jill's teacher uses good criticism. The teacher does *not* bawl out Jill for doing badly. The teacher does not say there is something wrong with Jill for having come up with an "F" paper.

Rather, the teacher meets with Jill and tries to help her understand how to do the computation. She might start out by being sympathetic. "Isn't it a shame that the grade is so poor when you worked so hard. You are an intelligent person. You can be a strong student. Perhaps it's just a little matter of not quite understanding how to do the problems. Why don't we go over a few together. Perhaps we'll see exactly where the trouble is." The teacher goes through several computations step-by-step until Jill understands the method of long division. Then the teacher says, "There, I knew you could do it. It was just the little business of moving that decimal."

Jill leaves feeling terrific. Of course she could do it. She knew how all along, except for that little problem with the decimal. And now that she has that under control, there's no question of her success. She's even anxious to take the next test to show off her long division prowess.

THREE ELEMENTS OF POSITIVE CRITICISM

There are three important features of positive criticism that you should notice in this example:

1. Notice that the nature of positive criticism in this school setting was to constantly *reinforce the value of the person.* Jill is a good person, a good student. The problem is shown to be external. The difficulty has to do with decimals. If Jill wants to get angry, she can get angry at the decimal point. That is what caused her problem and made her slip up.

The same holds true with workers. Positive criticism begins by assuming the worker *wants* to succeed and *can* succeed. The problem is something external that the employee can deal with. Once this has been established, then the employee has the confidence to move forward to correct whatever it might be.

2. Notice also that the problem that needs to be corrected is *always referred to as a MINOR difficulty.* There's an important reason for this. *Major* problems often don't have solutions. Minor problems, on the other hand, *always* can be solved. Making the difficulty "minor" automatically reinforces the belief that it can be overcome.

3. Finally we should notice that positive criticism always *engages the cooperation of the person being criticized.* It's not the teacher against the student, the manager against the worker. It's both working together to solve a common, solvable difficulty.

DOES IT WORK?

Now that we have some idea of what positive criticism is, the big question becomes, does it work?

Yes it does work, but don't expect to fully believe it yourself until you have a chance to try it out. In fact, part of the difficulty in believing that good criticism does work comes from the fact that it doesn't really fit the mold of what most of us consider as a definition of criticism.

As noted at the beginning of this chapter, with positive criticism we:

- ☐ Never bawl out another person
- ☐ Never are critical of the person
- ☐ Never reprimand
- ☐ Never are negative

It can be hard getting used to this new way of handling things, but the results are certainly worth it.

USING POSITIVE CRITICISM

Jimmy is a secretary whose responsibilities include answering phones, taking dictation, and writing letters. He answers the phones well, seems to be able to follow along with dictation, but there are frequently many misspelled words in letters he writes. Jimmy just can't spell.

He has just handed you the second letter for signing this morning and without even reading it, you can see that there are two glaring errors in the first line. Our immediate and natural impulse is to shout at Jimmy, "How did you ever get through school? Any dummy in the first grade can spell better than you can!"

However, you know that isn't positive criticism. It's a strong personal attack on Jimmy and he'll immediately recognize it as such. It probably won't improve his spelling and it will undoubtedly damage your ability to work with him. In fact, it might go so far as to reduce his efficiency in other areas.

Instead, you calm down. When there is a quiet moment, you call him aside. First, you reassure him of his overall performance. He's a good employee and does nearly all of his job well. He answers the phone politely and takes dictation accurately. There is, however, one small area that needs some improvement and you're quite confident he can handle it. You might even ask if he knows what you're talking about.

Of course he knows. Jimmy is well aware he can't spell.

If he knows, but isn't improving, perhaps it's because he doesn't understand the value of correct spelling. So you point out why good spelling is essential. Letters represent the company to others. If the letter has misspellings, it looks bad and then, so does the company. Further, Jimmy undoubtedly wants to succeed at his present job and move up. The inability to spell will surely slow him down. Therefore, it's to everyone's advantage if he simply gets over this minor thing of not spelling well.

Jimmy looks embarrassed. He doesn't know how to improve his spelling. Of course, you think to yourself, if he knew how to spell better, he would. So now you see to it that he learns how. You provide a pocket dictionary so that he can look up the words he's unsure of.

You allow him extra time for a while in writing letters so that he can use the dictionary. For a short period of time you might arrange to have another secretary (who knows how to spell), check Jimmy's work. You might even arrange for Jimmy to take a class at a local college in spelling improvement.

Will Jimmy spell better? Why shouldn't he? You want him to. He wants to himself. And now you've provided the means for him to improve.

AVOID BACK-SLIDING

You may be tempted to say, "But that's not criticism. Simply working with Jimmy never told him he was doing something very *badly*. There wasn't even any *punishment* for the letters he originally did poorly."

This sort of thinking is simply back-sliding. You've seen that negative criticism doesn't work. Yet, it's hard to shake the idea that criticism must be negative. So when you see positive (good) criticism at work without any negativism, you think it isn't criticism at all.

You must concentrate on your goal. Your goal is to correct and improve worker performance or behavior. If doing it this way works, then it is criticism. A little trick is to always avoid the following words when criticizing a worker:

KEY WORDS TO AVOID
WHEN CRITICIZING

Bad
Poor
Wrong
Punishment
Inadequate
Problem
Loser

THE DIFFERENCE BETWEEN CRITICISM AND REPRIMANDING

It's important to understand that there is a difference between criticizing and reprimanding. Criticism is typically used when we find someone doing a task or behaving incorrectly. It is used to *inform* the person and engage their *cooperation* in doing better.

Reprimanding, on the other hand, is used *after* criticism has been given a chance. You have used positive criticism; the person now understands how to do the task or how to behave correctly, but for some reason refuses. Reprimanding is now letting the person know that they are guilty of an infraction. (We'll discuss it more in the next chapter.)

HOW TO GIVE CONSTRUCTIVE CRITICISM

You need to be sure that you understand the procedure for giving good criticism. It isn't difficult and anyone can do it. It's just a matter of being aware of these five simple steps:

1. *Understand your goal:* What behavior or task do you want improved? To what level do you want it improved?

2. *Reassure the worker that this is not a personal attack:* It's the behavior that needs changing. Find and compliment the good work the person is doing, point out that you know the person can succeed, that he or she is basically a good worker.

3. *State that you have a* minor *but important concern:* Show confidence that the person can indeed improve and correct the situation.

4. *Determine how the problem can be corrected:* Discuss this with the worker and gain his or her cooperation.

5. *Reassure the worker:* Tell him or her that all will be well and to keep trying. In other words, point out that every opportunity still exists for success.

TASK 10

REPRIMANDING

*Most managers think reprimanding
is a coffee break without coffee.*

Project Director's comment

We reprimand when someone has done something wrong. Johnny is caught with his hand in the cookie jar. We give him a reprimand. Susy came to the dinner table without first washing her hands. She is reprimanded. Implicit in reprimanding is the understanding that both Johnny and Susy knew what was expected. They understood the correct behavior they were supposed to perform, but for some reason they did otherwise.

It's essentially the same in the workplace. John is tardy for work every day. If, in fact, he thoroughly understands that he is expected to be on time, then a reprimand may be in order. Susan makes a shambles of her work area. If she understands that because customers come through where she works, the area is expected to be neat, then a reprimand may be in order.

The goal of a reprimand is to let the worker know in no uncertain terms that:

☐ behavior or work (or both) is unacceptable
☐ what is acceptable work or behavior
☐ further infractions will not be tolerated

CRITICISM BEFORE REPRIMAND

Normally a reprimand will be preceded by criticism. As we said in the last chapter, the goal of criticism is to help and inform. An employee isn't achieving because he or she really doesn't know how. So you give constructive (positive) criticism which shows the person the path to success. On the other hand, if it is clear that the person already knows what to do (either in terms of behavior or work) and persists in not doing it, then it's a different matter.

It's important to understand that there is a thin line between reprimanding and criticizing. If you're not really sure that the person understands what's expected, then you should always strive for constructive criticism. *When in doubt, constructive criticism should always be used before reprimanding.* In fact many managers *never* reprimand. They always assume that a failure to do work correctly or to maintain correct behavior stems from a lack of understanding.

WHAT IS REPRIMANDING?

Reprimanding, like criticism, has negative connotations. It tells us that we've done something wrong. From childhood we tend to associate it with being bad.

This is unfortunate, for when people are told that they are bad, they tend to believe it. If you tell someone that he or she is a bad worker, then as their supervisor you have just defined his or her *value* as a worker—bad. If they weren't bad before, they certainly are going to lean that way now. After all, if your words are to be believed, it's what you expect of them.

The problem is that most people have been conditioned to thinking of being reprimanded as being attacked. *You* are not doing what's expected of you, hence there must be something wrong with *you*. (In fact the attack may be on the behavior, not the total person. We don't like what you *did*, not we don't like *you*. But that's not the way it usually comes across.)

BAD REPRIMANDING

Bad reprimanding, like bad criticism, makes a person feel diminished, a "bad person."

"This is the third time this week you've been late, John. What's the matter with you? Can't you hack it? You need to get your life in order. You can't expect to get here late all the time and not have people get angry with you."

People are very sensitive to your expectations of them. If John thinks you are "angry" with him, that you see his life as "out of order," then maybe that's the way he will act in the future. And since a person with a life out of order and people angry at him can't really be expected to come to work on time, maybe he won't in the future.

As with bad criticism, bad reprimanding is counterproductive. An attack on a person only makes that person less eager and less able to perform as you want. At times it may make your ego feel a little better, but a scolding simply isn't going to get the results you want. (And, after all, what you are ultimately concerned about is results.)

GOOD REPRIMANDING

The key to good reprimanding is expectation. If you expect bad work or behavior, very likely you'll get it. If you expect good work or behavior, then that's the result you're most likely to see.

When you give a constructive reprimand, behind it must be your assumption that you are dealing with a good person who can and will correct the offending behavior or work. If you don't believe in the person, then you really have no business reprimanding. If you think the person is bad, all you'll be doing is reinforcing this belief, making things worse for the person and, very likely, worse also for yourself.

If you have a positive attitude toward a worker who

is not performing as required, if you believe the person wants to succeed, then your reprimand will take a constructive form.

Susan's work area is a mess. You go to Susan and say you know she's aware that because of her sensitive location in front of customers, it's vital her work station be kept neat and tidy. Yet, three times this week the station hasn't been that way.

"We have confidence in you and your abilities and believe you can succeed in the company. However, one of your job requirements is a neat work station. If you can't maintain tidiness, then that job requirement isn't being fulfilled and we may not be able to continue you in this job.

"It's just a simple matter of neatness, which can easily and quickly be corrected. I know you're a good worker and you'll take care of it."

The good or constructive reprimand begins and ends on a positive note.

THREE PARTS OF A CONSTRUCTIVE REPRIMAND

There are three essential elements that must be present in a good constructive reprimand:

1. The person must be made to feel that it is only a single identifiable aspect of the work or behavior that is the problem. It's not *the person* that's wrong. It's one *small* thing he or she is doing.

2. The worker must believe that the problem is correctable and that once corrected, everything will be well again. In other words, once the problem is taken care of, it will once again be possible for the worker to move

forward with achievements in the company. (If this possibility isn't there, why should the worker correct the problem?)

3. The employee must understand that there will be consequences if the problem is not corrected.

CONSEQUENCES

While it is important to point out the need for compliance when a worker is not performing, it is equally important to underline the fact that continued lack of performance will have a consequence. In other words, only if the worker fully understands that you will be forced to do something (such as write a poor evaluation, transfer, fine, or fire them) is the reprimand likely to have teeth.

Making consequences for bad performance has two benefits. First, it makes the worker responsible for solving the problem. Second, it makes sure that the worker understands that it's his or her problem, not yours. It's important that the problem be identified as the worker's. Giving consequences allows you to be very up-front with the worker. Here's the job. You know what's expected. It's up to you to do it or you'll have to pay the cost.

The key to remember about consequences is this rule:

Workers must be made to understand that they are responsible for performance.

If they don't perform, undesirable consequences are inevitable.

WHEN TO REPRIMAND

A reprimand should be given only if the offense is either serious or repeated.

John is tardy once in awhile, but his work is complete and on time. No reprimand is needed. Just look the other way. John may need the flexibility of occasionally coming in late in order to maintain his work load.

Susan's desk is occasionally a mess, but she cleans it up right away if any customers are present and always speaks to them in a friendly and warm manner. Forget the desk. Perhaps some of her work is difficult and frustrating for her and that is reflected once in a while in her work station's appearance. As long as she's getting the job done, overlook an occasional lapse in neatness.

Simply being aware that some problems are occasional and are not serious can save you enormous headaches. Learning to live with a few little quirks of your workers is one of the requirements of being a manager.

Richard, a vital member of an engineering team, is late in turning in his report. His tardiness causes other members of the team to be put behind schedule and this holds up the entire project. If after constructive criticism the behavior continues a reprimand is certainly in order.

Helen is required to keep a daily tab of all transactions. It must be completed by closing time, but several times she has taken long lunch hours and been unable to finish. She has left work at the end of the day with the work uncompleted. This puts the company at risk with the regulators. A criticism after the first offense is in order. If it happens again, a reprimand is then called for.

Serious offenses are those which jeopardize other workers or the company, in other words those which have a bad effect on results. Repeated serious offenses always call for a reprimand.

GET IT IN WRITING

It is important to understand that a reprimand can sometimes be the first step on the road to dismissal of an employee. As can be seen in the section on firing, it is therefore vital that a "paper trail" be established. One of the worst things that can happen is to attempt to fire an employee, only to have that person say, "You never told me I wasn't doing my job. You never gave me a chance to improve." This can have serious implications.

If you reprimand someone and only the two of you are present, then it is only your word against theirs that the reprimand actually took place. What carries more weight is if after a reprimand you write a memo and send a copy to the person. Even more weight is carried if a copy of that memo is put in the worker's permanent file. The most weight comes when you have the worker sign a copy of the memo indicating that they've seen it, and then put that in their file.

Some managers use the following rule of thumb (although it is certainly not foolproof). They give no written memos for a criticism or a first reprimand. Everything after that, however, is documented in writing.

The advantage of written documentation of a reprimand is that at some later date, if there is a dispute over whether or not a warning was given, the paper record will usually be believed over oral recall.

HOW TO REPRIMAND

The most important part of reprimanding is being sure the worker understands what is happening. Now that we've seen what reprimands are and when they should be used, let's see how that statement works.

In our experience a typical faulty reprimand goes something like this. Sam, the manager, is upset with Gil's work performance. He has already constructively criticized Gil. The performance hasn't improved. Now it's time for the reprimand.

Sam calls Gil into his office, and asks him to sit down. Then the manager says, "How's the wife and kids?"

Gil nods that they are fine.

Sam, the manager, says, "You like the work here? You've done good work for us in the past."

Gil nods and smiles.

Sam fidgets with his tie, then says, "I've been watching your work recently." He looks up to see if Gil is following. Gil nods that he is waiting.

Sam continues. "It's not bad, but I'm sure it'll improve."

Gil nods indicating he's also sure.

Sam says, "Well, I'm certainly glad to hear that. You're one of our top employees. I'm sure you'll go far in the company." He shakes Gil's hand.

Gil leaves the office feeling terrific. The boss just called him in to give him a compliment on his performance. He even feels good enough to take the rest of the day off.

CONFRONTATION

The problem, of course, is that Sam never really reprimanded Gil. Gil, in fact, never knew there had been a reprimand.

Why?

It's a problem of confrontation. Any time you have to tell someone something they don't want to hear, you are going to get "bad vibrations" from them. They aren't going to be thrilled to learn that they might be fired if they don't change. That fact isn't going to make this one of their best days. You know, too, that some people react to bad news in disturbing ways. They might:

Yell
Argue
Cry
Plead
Become physical

None of the above is something you want to experience and, fearing a confrontation, you may end up giving faulty reprimands. Too often the worker never knows he or she has been reprimanded.

AVOIDING CONFRONTATION

While you can never be 100 percent sure how a worker will take a reprimand, you should remember two things. First, as a manager, you must sometimes give reprimands. Second, if the reprimand is constructive (if it contains the three basic elements), a bad confrontation is much less likely to occur.

Remember, the three elements to a constructive reprimand are:

☐ Reprimand not the person, but the identifiable problem part of the work.

☐ Show how to correct the problem and achieve future success.

☐ Let the worker know there are undesirable consequences for continued bad performance.

A bad reprimand is bad. But a faulty reprimand is like none at all. Give constructive reprimands, but be sure the worker fully understands he or she is being reprimanded.

TASK 11

GIVING PROMOTIONS AND BONUSES

*Money is a good servant,
but a bad master.*

Quoted by Bacon

A bonus should be given only as a reward for superior performance. A promotion should be given only when a worker has outgrown his or her present responsibilities and is ready to take on new ones. That is the ideal. Actual practice, however, is often far different.

BONUSES

There are many different kinds of bonuses. The most common is the regular year-end bonus offered by many companies. Some companies, however, offer bonuses for everything from recruiting new personnel to having top sales.

While we have no qualms about specialized bonuses, we feel the year-end bonus is probably the most misused in the country. To see why, we need to understand what the real purpose of a bonus is.

SPECIALIZED BONUSES

Pete manages a production line and for the last six months he has exceeded his quota. It is through his diligent efforts that the increased production has come about. One way the company can recognize his achievement is through a bonus (cash, company stock, or a prize). This lets Pete know he's appreciated. It also spurs him—and other workers—on to greater achievements.

Sally sells more houses than anyone else in the office during the month of August. As a reward she receives a free week's vacation in Hawaii. This is a sales bonus. Often announced in advance, it encourages salespeople to work harder and it rewards the hardest worker. (Frequently there are second- and third-place prizes to console those who also achieved, but did not win.)

The purpose of these specialized bonuses is to encourage and reward achievement. When the bonus is for a specific accomplishment, it is almost always effective. In the above examples, increased production and higher sales were directly related to the bonus.

YEAR-END BONUSES

Regular year-end bonuses are quite a different matter. Many companies, particularly large institutional ones, regularly reward workers at the end of the year with a bonus that can sometimes be as much as 10 percent or more of the worker's annual salary. Typically such bonuses are awarded across-the-board during good years. The company made money, the workers are the company, therefore the workers should be rewarded.

While the logic seems compelling, it is flawed. The company may have made money because of economic conditions totally unrelated to its workers' performance. A new and unexpected demand for the company's product may have been totally responsible for increased profits. Why, therefore, should the workers be rewarded?

The converse also may be true. A company may run into a few lean years. The workers (and managers) could be contributing outstanding achievements. Yet external factors such as unfavorable exchange rates or a recession could stifle demand. The company loses money, hence there are no year-end bonuses. Yet, shouldn't those workers who had extraordinary achievement be recognized with a reward?

The economics of business often make year-end bonuses either gratuitous or impossible to give. Both situations are bad in the workplace.

What does a worker think if he or she has slacked off all year and still receives a bonus because the company in general did well. Is this worker encouraged to greater achievement or does the bonus do the opposite—encourage continued mediocrity?

Or what does a worker feel who has put forth great effort and has achieved all the goals and more that were outlined for him or her, and then does not receive an anticipated financial reward because the company in general is doing poorly?

Even more difficult, what about a worker who has fallen into a pattern of receiving bonuses every year? If a bonus has been given every year for the last three years, then on the fourth year it's expected. It's come to be thought of as a part of regular wages. If a bonus *isn't* paid, the worker is going to feel as if something due wasn't given. He or she is going to feel angry or insulted, and will probably end up taking out those feelings in the work.

Ultimately the problem with year-end bonuses is that they don't do what they are supposed to do. They don't act as rewards. Either they end up being undeserved windfalls or they produce hard feelings.

We encourage you, as a manager, to reconsider your policy with regard to bonuses. We recommend instituting specific bonuses for recognized achievements. Timing should be considered more important than simply giving "regular" bonuses. This may enormously improve the productivity of your workers and your company.

PROMOTIONS

Promotions are often given as rewards, sometimes in lieu of bonuses. Archie does well at his present job, so we'll reward him by moving him up.

The effect, of course, has often been described as the "Peter Principle" (from the book of the same name by Laurence J. Peters). Workers are rewarded with repeated promotions until they reach a level of incompetence. When they finally reach a job they can't handle, they remain there hurting the company, or they are embarrassingly shuffled to the side.

It is vital to understand that promotions should *never* be given as rewards. Only praise and bonuses should be given as rewards for good work.

Promotions should be given for two reasons:

1. A worker has outgrown his or her present job and is ready for new responsibilities.

2. A worker is not doing well at the present job, yet there is another at which he or she might succeed. (A transfer.)

The rule is simple. *Reward achievement with a bonus; promote to get greater achievement.*

TASK 12

MANAGING
PAY
CUTS
AND
DEMOTIONS

For our next reorganization . . .

C.E.O's opening
statement at a
full staff meeting

P ay cuts and demotions are two very difficult areas for managers to handle. Nobody likes to cut a worker's pay. No one likes to hand out a demotion. tion. Nevertheless, they are both things with which some managers must deal. Pay cuts and demotions come about for various reasons. Sometimes, much to the chagrin of the manager, the company simply must cut back. Rather than fire personnel, pay cuts and demotions are handed round. We'll look into handling these shortly. In other cases, however, pay cuts and demotions are given as punishment for bad performance.

AS PUNISHMENT

Our feeling is that pay cuts or demotions used as punishment are counterproductive. Sidney is simply not doing his job. His manager decides to demote him one level with a corresponding cut in pay.

What was the manager's goal? Probably it was to get Sidney to perform better. Will the demotion result in increased performance? Unlikely. Sidney is sure to be angered, perhaps outraged and infuriated, by what happened. In retaliation he will probably *decrease* his productivity.

If, as a manager, you are concerned that a person isn't performing as desired, don't think pay cuts or demotion. Instead look into the chapters in this book on encouraging, criticizing, and reprimanding. Use the techniques described there to get your goals accomplished.

A worker demoted or given a pay cut for punishment is like a wounded animal. He or she just lingers around the company bleeding on others.

AS A TRANSFER

If the worker is not able to handle the work, consider transferring the person to another position. A transfer to a more suitable job, even one with a lesser title and lesser pay, can frequently result in a turnaround in worker performance, as long as it's handled constructively.

DIFFERENCE BETWEEN
PUNISHMENT AND TRANSFER

A pay cut and demotion as punishment often leaves the worker doing essentially the same task, but with fewer responsibilities and less money. This frequently results in resentment.

A transfer, if handled constructively, puts the worker in a new position (albeit with lesser pay and perhaps fewer or different responsibilities). The new position, however, can be viewed as a "second chance" or as a new opportunity. It may result in improved performance.

AS A NECESSITY

Sometimes we have no choice in demoting and reducing pay. The company may be enduring hard times. Sales and income are down. Survival is at stake, and the only way the company can survive as a whole is by cutting back salaries and demoting some workers. This is a trying situation, but one which sometimes can be managed surprisingly well. Many companies, particularly in recent years, have weathered such adverse conditions with nary a loss in personnel.

The key is the method by which the pay cuts and/or

demotions are handled. If the worker is made to understand the problem and to feel that he or she is not being singled out, then cooperation can usually be expected. In fact, sometimes such cut-backs can result in increased enthusiasm and productivity from workers.

There are three rules to follow which usually produce good results from unavoidable pay cuts and/or demotions.

1. COMMUNICATION

Be sure the workers understand what the problem is and that it's real. They must believe that belt-tightening is currently the *only* possible solution.

A good method of communicating this information is through informal meetings and round-table discussions. Such settings give the workers as well as the managers a voice. Typically the managers present the problems. Then the workers are given full opportunity to express their grievances (which they surely will have). Finally management says something such as, "Yes, you are right. It is a shame. But it's what we have to do."

This is an invitation for the workers to offer alternatives, which they surely will. Patience is the order of the day here. Each alternative must be explored to demonstrate that it really won't work. Ultimately, if in fact it really is the case, everyone at the meeting will be forced to see that pay cuts and/or demotions are really necessary for survival.

2. EQUALITY

Once the workers see the necessity for belt-tightening, it is helpful if they understand that everyone will suffer equally. It can't be that one worker takes a pay cut while another doesn't (or what's worse, gets a raise!). It is also helpful if cuts are across-the-board, taken not just by workers, but by management as well. This is a particularly useful argument when dealing with labor unions.

All must believe they are in the same lifeboat if necessitated pay cuts and/or demotions are not to destroy a company. If even one manager or executive is seen as floating luxuriously in a yacht, *everyone* will scramble to get aboard and the lifeboat will be upset and sunk.

3. SWIFTNESS

If pay cuts and/or demotions are really needed, don't delay instituting them. Once workers are convinced of the necessity, move forward at once. Any delay will certainly be taken as evidence that the belt-tightening really isn't necessary. After all, if the company can afford to wait, then things can't really be as bad as reported.

ALTERNATIVES

Sometimes it may be possible to sweeten the blow of a forced pay cut or demotion. Workers, for example, could be offered company stock. Another alternative is to agree to bonuses once the company's health returns. The pay cuts/demotions can be made to appear as a trade-off. Take less now, but get more later on.

Of course, these techniques have limited application. A worker can't take unsaleable stock to the grocery store, or bank future "iffy" bonuses. Nevertheless, sometimes the offer itself is worth more than what is offered.

TASK 13

DECIDING
TO
FIRE

*We've never fired anyone—our
former employees fired themselves!*

General Manager of
a computer sales firm

T here is nothing more difficult for most managers to do than to fire a worker. Firing implies failure. It also often results in guilt on the part of the manager. Many think, "What right have I to ruin this person's life by firing him?"

As troublesome as firing may be, it is nevertheless sometimes a necessity. In this chapter we'll look into the decision process involved in firing. We'll also examine some of the steps you may want to take as a manager to ease the risks of firing and to make it more palatable.

REASONS FOR FIRING

It's important to understand that there are different reasons for firing and these require different kinds of decisions.

For example, a manager may have an excellent worker for whom he has nothing but praise and hope. But because of economic conditions he must dismiss the employee. Here the firing decision is made either directly by someone else or directly by economic necessity. Either way, it is a difficult task. But at least from a decision viewpoint, there is little room for the manager to maneuver.

In many cases, however, the situation is that a worker simply cannot function in his or her current job. The firing decision now becomes entirely the manager's. He must decide whether to keep the worker on in the hopes of improvement, or immediately fire. We'll have much more to say about deciding on forced firings in the next few paragraphs.

In some cases, the necessity of terminating employment may be apparent to both the worker and the manager. There is no great confrontation and little emotional distress. The worker leaves on his or her own and parts friends with the manager. This, as we'll see, is the ideal method of firing.

ALTERNATIVES TO FIRING

As part of the decision process it's important to consider whether there are alternatives to firing. The most common alternative is a transfer.

Patricia was hired to do accounting work. She was a bright, outgoing young woman who loved to talk with people. Unfortunately this worked against her. Instead of focusing her mind on her books, she would chat with whoever came by her desk. Her warm friendly manner soon made her extremely popular with the other workers. Unfortunately, her work was dismal. It soon became apparent that Patricia was not going to be able to handle the accounting job. Her manager gave her objectives, encouraged, criticized, and even reprimanded her. She wanted to do the work, but her personality was just not suited to it.

Faced with firing this charming young woman, the manager actively sought an alternative. It turned out that there was an opening for a person to handle receptionist and billing work in another part of the company. The manager talked with Patricia about a transfer. It meant a step-down in pay. However, Patricia knew she wasn't doing well and felt terrible about her current work. The transfer seemed like a second chance and she grabbed for it. If things worked out, within six months she'd be making as much as she was as an accountant.

Patricia was a star at her new job. She was a whiz at billing, with her accounting background, and she had plenty of opportunity to chat as a receptionist.

In this case an alternative that made sense all around was found. Other alternatives involve giving the problem worker more responsibility (or taking some away if the person has too much). So called "self-starters" need a free rein to achieve. Give them control over their work and they may blossom. Alternately, a rote worker may need to have more supervision.

The point is that even within a particular job, transferring the direction of the work to more accurately suit the temperament of the employee may be a realistic alternative to firing.

If you look carefully, you may find many other alternatives in your own work situation.

MOVING TO THE SIDE

It's important to distinguish between a realistic transfer, such as indicated above, and moving a worker to the side. A transfer as a realistic alternative gives the employee a second chance in a more suitable job where he or she can succeed. "Moving to the side" simply sends the worker to another job out of the manager's way where he or she isn't likely to get into trouble (or to succeed). This moves the worker into a "non-job" where the person simply exists without hope of achievement.

Moving a worker to the side usually occurs when a manager doesn't have the courage or the ability to fire outright and doesn't want to take the time to try to arrange a creative transfer. Joan wants to get rid of James, but she just can't bear the emotional confrontation of a firing. So instead, she "promotes" him into a useless job.

He has been pushed off to the side. He may have little to no responsibilities and duties. There is no contribution he can make. He simply sits there, an embarrassment to both himself and the company. It's humiliating for James. Taking away the possibility of achievement robs him of motivation and he gets depressed and becomes morose. Joan feels sorry for him, but because she doesn't have the heart to fire him, she lets him dangle there indefinitely.

Moving an employee to the side destroys morale all around and should be avoided. It is always better to fire outright and give the person a chance to succeed elsewhere than to have an empty shell hanging around the company.

FIRING AS A MANAGEMENT FAILURE

There's an old maxim that is frequently quoted in teaching: "There are no student failures, there are only teacher failures." Translated to the workplace it would read, "There are no worker failures, there are only management failures." Of course, there are times when things don't work out and it's not the manager's fault. A worker can have personal problems. A manager can inherit a bad worker. Or there may simply be irreconcilable personality differences between the worker and the manager.

But generally speaking, the manager has great opportunity to bring workers along. If the management job is done right—beginning with hiring correctly—then there really shouldn't be many worker failures. You should be able to develop and build successful employees.

On the other hand, if it turns out that you're faced with firing many people, you should perhaps look at your own management performance. Perhaps there's something that you're doing wrong that needs to be corrected. Maybe your management technique is at fault.

Perhaps the failure really isn't so much in the workers as it is in yourself.

THE IDEAL IN FIRING

Hennesey was an old and experienced manager. He had been with the company for over fifteen years and had supervised hundreds of workers. Yet, though employees had come and gone, Hennesey had actually fired only a handful during the entire time. Mostly, the bad workers quit on their own.

One day the president of the company called Hennesey in and asked for his secret. "You have a way with workers. How do you avoid firing?"

Hennesey sat back in his chair and put it as simply as he could. "I don't need to fire. When a worker sees that he can't do the job, he fires himself."

The president of the company was intrigued. "When they see they can't do the job? What do you mean? How do they see that?"

Hennesey seemed surprised by the president's questions. "It's quite simple. If Joyce is working for me, she knows what the job involves. We both clearly understand the performance required and the objectives. We both work toward her achieving success. If she can't succeed here for some reason that neither of us can control, then it's only natural for her to want to move to another place where she can succeed. She knows that what I want most is her success."

"Yes, I think I see." said the president. "Only what if she's afraid of not being able to find other work? What if she's satisfied just hanging on even without success? Or what if she doesn't care that you know she's failing? Don't you have to take action then?"

Hennesey looked puzzled. "Perhaps we're having a communication failure. When I said she knew I wanted her to succeed, I didn't mean to limit that to this job. True, I want her to know my own success at work will only come about through her work success. It's mainly because of this that she trusts me and works with me.

"But she also knows I want her to succeed not only at this job at this time and place, but in her life as well. I want her to be a successful person.

"Once she understands that, that I'm really on her side, then it's very hard for her to continue on here in a mode of failure. If she's afraid about finding another job, I'll help her overcome her fear. I'll help her look for other work. If she's just hanging on repeatedly failing, then I'll know that she has some sort of psychological problem and try to get her to seek counseling. People don't normally seek failure, they seek success and achievement. As long as I keep that as the cornerstone of my relationship with her, I can't go far wrong.

"If she knows that her success is first in my mind, she has to care about what I think. I encourage her to achieve and she is motivated to do just that, if not at this company, then somewhere else."

"Remarkable," the president said. "And it always works?"

"No, of course not. I'm far from perfect. I have my own problems and my own needs. Sometimes I really don't think about Joyce, about my workers first. Sometimes I make mistakes and fail as a manager. And sometimes I just can't establish rapport with a worker. In those cases I may have to fire.

"But I understand the ideal and work toward it."

The "ideal" which Hennesey sought is, of course, having workers who are sufficiently motivated to seek success that when it becomes apparent they aren't finding it at his company, they immediately move elsewhere. These workers aren't looking to get by loafing through the day or to get fired and live on unemployment compensation for a few months.

Ideally we hire workers who wanted to achieve. Ideally we build on this motivation. If for some reason they don't achieve, then they should be sufficiently motivated to remove themselves from the current workplace and find another where they can achieve.

Of course, even as Hennesey understood, the ideal is something to aim at. We don't always achieve it. Even Hennesey, with all his experience, sometimes wasn't successful. On occasions even he had to fire his failures.

MAKING THE FIRING DECISION

When firing for cause, the decision comes down to two choices: Can you keep this employee, work with him or her to improve their work or behavior, *or* should you fire, hire someone else, and start over?

There's an old maxim that goes, "The evil we know is always preferrable to the evil that we haven't encountered."

We feel that if there is any way you can get involved with the worker to achieve improvement, then you should make the attempt. A bad worker transformed into a good worker is an enormous plus both to the company and to the manager. Nothing looks better on your record than to be able to take a liability and turn it into an asset.

On the other hand, it is important to be realistic:

☐ Is the worker unable to handle the job even with additional training?
☐ Does he or she not have the right temperament for the work?
☐ Is this the wrong person for the job?

If your answer to any of the above questions is "yes," then you ought to seriously consider firing.

TASK 14

FIRING:
PROCEDURE
AND
DOCUMENTATION

*Our employees know where
they stand with the company
at all times—and that
includes when they're fired!*

Owner/Manager of a
small accounting firm

A few years ago, firing at worst might have been an emotionally trying episode. Today, not only can there be emotional distress, but a firing can also result in litigation and financial damages to a company. Lawsuits charging discrimination or wrongful firing are being filed with increasing regularity throughout the country.

As a result, it is becoming increasingly difficult to fire an employee, particularly in large companies or those involved with any kind of government work. In some companies, in fact, passing the probationary period means the employee is virtually immune to firing except for severe cause. (Almost no one is immune to layoff, of course.) Nevertheless, it is still possible to fire an employee for cause in most situations provided the proper paperwork has been done. In this chapter we're going to look at some of the procedures and documentation that may be needed to fire.

Special Note: Rules relating to firing vary from state to state and related laws are constantly changed or reinterpreted. Therefore, no guarantee or assurance is given by the authors that the following material will be applicable to any specific firing situation. The reader should not rely on this material. Before firing, you should seek competent legal counsel to make you aware of your rights and responsibilities.

WHO YOU CAN'T FIRE

In some states it is possible to fire at will. That means that no particular cause or reason is needed. (California is one such state.) A manager simply decides to fire an individual and does not have to have a specific reason.

In other states an employer can only fire for cause.

There must be a good reason for firing. In all states, however, most employers may not fire for prejudice.

ANTI-DISCRIMINATION

This is widely understood today, but a few additional descriptive words won't hurt. Prejudice involves a broad area of laws that protect workers. Basically the same antidiscrimination rules that protect workers from hiring discrimination also protect them from firing discrimination. (See Task 5.)

Additionally, if a firing changes the overall status of a protected group in an affirmative action situation, firing may also be difficult. (For example, firing a minority worker might affect the overall representation of minorities in the company.)

FAIRNESS

There is a broad area that is open to interpretation that is generally considered to fall under the category of "fairness." It is also frequently called "Wrongful discharge." In many states an employer is required in general to deal fairly with employees. Unfair dealing can result in a fired worker having a claim against a manager and his or her company.

Fairness has many interpretations. For example, a worker cannot normally be fired for taking off work for jury duty. Such a firing might be construed as a wrongful discharge.

Similarly, a company cannot fire an individual who refuses to break the law. A manager wants to be sure deliveries are made on time, so he demands his workers get from one destination to another in so many hours. But doing so requires the workers to drive faster than the legal speed limit. A worker fired for refusing to meet the time requirements by breaking the speeding law might have a case under the fairness doctrine.

Additionally there is the matter of company policy. If the company has a stated policy with regard to firing practices and the manager violates that policy in the firing, the worker could have a claim. Similarly, if the worker has given good service for a long period of time, it may be unfair to arbitrarily fire him or her.

A manager can also get into trouble if the worker can demonstrate that the firing was for bad cause. This could involve *retaliation* for something the worker did. Or the worker might say that there was a contract (written or implied) that the firing violated.

Fairness requires that the manager shows good faith when firing workers.

PROBATIONARY VS. "PERMANENT" EMPLOYEES

Many companies have a "probationary" period to allow both worker and manager a trial period to see how things work out. If the worker is able to handle the job, then "permanent" status is conferred after the end of a probationary period. If the worker is unable to perform as required, then it is understood that he or she may be dismissed.

It's possible for a company to get into trouble because it refers to its non-probationary employees as "permanent" workers. The word "permanent" of itself suggests that the job is guaranteed. Perhaps better words to use would be "regular" or "non-probationary" employees.

Many managers make the mistake of thinking that firing can be done automatically to any probationary worker. This is not usually the case. Probationary workers are also protected under anti-discrimination and fairness rules. This means that similar documentation and procedures are often required for firing a probationary person as for firing a regular employee.

This is not to say, however, that firing of probationary employees is as difficult as firing regular employees. It's not. In some states where cause is required for firing a regular employee, no cause may be required for firing a probationary one. Additionally, it is usually not difficult to substantiate poor performance in a probationary employee, while this may be more difficult for a regular employee. Finally, there is usually far less paperwork involved in firing a probationary worker.

PROBLEMS IN FIRING A REGULAR EMPLOYEE

Special problems arise when a manager tries to fire a regular employee. These problems stem from the fact that once an employee has passed through the probationary period, he or she has indirectly been given the company's stamp of approval.

Some managers really don't perceive what the difficulties are here. They feel that if the person isn't performing the job or if their behavior isn't suitable, then he or she should be fired.

Fairness, however, requires that you consider not only the employee's immediate performance, but performance over their whole period of employment. It also requires that you consider any promises given and expectations aroused. Finally it insists that you let the person know what the problem is and give them an opportunity to correct it.

For example, Sammy is not currently performing well. His manager, Hazel, has gone through the various tasks from encouragement through criticism to reprimanding. She has explained what's wrong and given him a chance to correct it. But for the past six months, Sammy just hasn't done any work, so Hazel wants to fire him.

But Sammy has been with the company for ten years. During that time he received regular pay increases and promotions. He has even received one or two commendations for his efforts on special projects. Written reports by his previous managers have been filled with praise. In addition, when the subject of termination is broached, Sammy protests that in the past he has been promised a "job for as long as you want it."

Finally, Sammy points to other workers who have been with the company who have had periods when they were having trouble and yet weren't fired. He knows one worker, Cal, who slacked off for nearly two years without being discharged.

Hazel has her work cut out for her. If she attempts to fire, Sammy may come back with a wrongful discharge claim. He can point to:

1. Good past performance with a record of positive reviews and even commendations.

2. Approval from the company in the form of pay raises and promotions and a promise of employment regardless of effort.

3. Company history of not firing others who had the same offense.

On the basis of Sammy's past ten years, promises made, and expectations aroused, Hazel does not have much of a case, *unless* she can clearly document his current bad performance and demonstrate that firing him falls within set company procedures.

EXTENDING THE PROBATIONARY PERIOD

Because of the problems involved in firing a regular employee, some companies try to extend the probationary period. In some cases, it is done in stages. The first stage may last three months, the second stage six months, and the last stage a year. In other companies, there is no clearly defined probationary period. The attempt is made to give the appearance that workers are on probation from the time they are hired for as long as they are with the company. Such undefined probation has little real meaning and is of questionable validity.

DRUG ABUSE

A special area of firing which involves both regular and probationary workers comes under the heading of drug or substance abuse. This is an increasing problem.

Absenteeism, rowdiness, and inability to perform work can often be directly related to the consumption of alcohol or other drugs. In most companies, obvious or repeated drunkenness or overt drug abuse is considered a reason for firing.

However, this may not be as easy as it seems. Alcoholism, for example, is today widely considered a disease. In many areas a worker cannot be fired because he or she has an illness. Therefore, drunkenness by itself may not be a sufficient cause for firing. (In addition, the worker might claim that the work itself drove him or her to drink!)

To get rid of a habitually drunk employee, the manager may first need to make an attempt to correct the problem. Many companies today offer alcohol and drug rehabilitation programs and counseling through established medical clinics. A worker with a drug-related problem may need to be offered help, not forced into unemployment.

Only if the worker refuses the rehabilitation and counseling or is repeatedly not helped by it *and* is unable to perform his or her job, may firing then become a realistic possibility.

HAVING A FIRING PROCEDURE

In order to effectively fire a worker, it is usually advisable for the company to have a set firing procedure. This consists of a series of steps that are to be taken before any employee is fired. This firing procedure is usually written out and is made available to employees, sometimes in a company manual.

There are at least two advantages to having an established firing procedure. The first is that it clearly states the steps that must be taken. A manager thus knows what he or she must do in order to fire a worker. The worker, too, is also made aware of the steps. This means that if the steps are followed, the worker cannot claim that the firing came as a surprise or that it went against company policy.

Additionally, a firing procedure avoids the claim that one worker was given preferential treatment over another. If the procedure is followed in *every* case, then a worker can't claim that a manager let a similar problem go by with another employee.

A TYPICAL PROCEDURE

The actual procedure used by your company is important, but perhaps more so is simply having one that is used regularly.

The following is a typical firing procedure. It is certainly not applicable in all cases. But, it should give an idea of what a firing procedure looks like:

Step 1: Regular reviews, with the worker's problems clearly stated. Salary increases, bonuses, or promotions might be withheld on the basis of these reviews.

Step 2: Criticism

Step 3: Oral Reprimand

Step 4: Written Reprimand(s). The number of reprimands required may vary.

Step 5: Written warning(s) that the worker must correct problem or may be fired. (Number of warnings given may vary.)

Step 6: Suspension for a short period with pay. This could be to give the worker time to reconsider performance or it may be for the purpose of investigating the worker's difficulties.

Step 7: Written notice of job termination presented in person to the worker.

Notice that the firing procedure has a definite pattern. That pattern is based on informing the worker each step of the way that there is a problem and what's involved in correcting it. Each step of the way the worker may improve performance and thus stop the procedure. The procedure is continued only if the worker's performance continues to be unacceptable.

A good rule to remember with a firing procedure is that *it should be fair, informative, and firm*. Additionally, the procedure should emphasize that *the problem is with performance, not with the person*.

DOCUMENTATION

Documentation means creating and saving a written record. Some call this a "paper trail." Essentially, it means following the steps of the firing procedure in writing. Documenting is a tiresome, troublesome job most people would prefer to avoid. Consequently, we tend to ask ourselves, "Do I really need to bother documenting this?"

The answer is YES!

Of course, if the worker does not protest the firing and no problems result, there really is no need for documentation. However, if there is a protest, a lawsuit, or a claim with an arbitration board, then virtually the *only* thing that can back up a firing is written documentation. Since when you fire you can never know in advance if there is or is not going to be a problem, the rule is to *always document every firing*.

WHAT TO DOCUMENT

Asking what it is necessary to document is like asking, "What tax papers should I save in the event of an IRS audit?" One answer is, save everything. You never know what the IRS will ask about. In the case of firing, the same rule may apply. Document everything because you never know what will turn out to be important later on.

ITEMS COMMONLY DOCUMENTED
The following items are commonly documented:

Reprimands
Reviews
Warnings
Suspensions
Any disciplinary action
Notice of termination of employment

WHAT TO INCLUDE
IN DOCUMENTATION

On each document there are certain basic items that should be included. Not including them may not be fatal, but their inclusion adds strength to the document.

POINT
The document should state what it is. If it's a reprimand, then it should say so. If it's a warning, then that should be clearly stated. This avoids a worker coming back later on and saying that he or she was given a piece of paper, but didn't know what it meant. Putting the *point* of the document right in the heading is a good idea. In addition, you should state where in the overall procedure this document fits in.

PERSON, PLACE, TIME, AND DATE
The name of the worker, the job title, the name of the manager, and any other relevant information regarding

the person should be included. The place the document was handed out as well as the time can also be included. In addition the time of the problem (or the period during which it occurred) as well as where it occured can be mentioned as can other persons involved.

PROBLEM
The document should clearly state what the problem is. If the worker is not performing duties, it should explain (A) what is expected; (B) how the worker is not performing; (C) how the lack of performance is affecting the company (such as lost sales, slowdowns, etc.).

REMEDIATION
The worker must be given a chance to improve. The manager should explain the steps for improvement (if any) agreed upon with the worker and the timeframe for improvement. The document should clearly explain the consequences if performance does not improve. (If there was no agreement, the manager should explain why not and what further action is contemplated.)

SIGNATURE
This is perhaps the most vital part of the document. It's one thing to put a piece of paper in a worker's file. It's quite another thing, later on in front of an arbitrator or judge, to prove that the worker actually saw that document (or a copy of it). The problem is solved, of course, if the worker signs that they have seen the document. Then there can really be no doubts.

A worker should be asked to sign a copy of the document. Sometimes right above the signature can be a statement saying that you and the worker came to an agreement and by signing, the worker agrees to abide by what was decided.

That's the ideal. In the real world, however, workers may well refuse to sign such a statement. Since what's important is only to prove that the worker actually saw the document, it may be possible to get him or her to sign something else. For example, it could be a simple statement that the worker received a copy and had a chance to read the document.

If all else fails, another manager might be called in to witness that the worker was given the document, had a chance to read it, and agreed to abide by it. That other manager might now sign as a witness.

TIMEFRAME

From what's been said thus far, you may get the impression that firing is a long, drawn-out procedure. Unfortunately, in today's world, that is often true. To fire a regular employee can often take six months or longer.

What's usually involved is taking enough time to build the documentation necessary to fire. The following time chart gives a rough idea of how long this might be. (Of course, all of the items should be documented in the worker's file, as shown at the top of page 146.)

PITFALLS TO AVOID

We've already suggested many of the pitfalls that a manager could get into, but there are some others that bear special attention.

FAILURE TO SUPERVISE
DURING PROBATION

Managers tend to be rather busy people. There are lots of things to do and time is frequently very tight. There-

REVIEW
(STATING INADEQUATE PERFORMANCE)

CRITICISM
1 MONTH

REPRIMAND(S)
2 TO 8 WEEKS

WARNING(S)
1 TO 4 WEEKS

SUSPENSION
(FOR PURPOSES OF CONSIDERING
IMPROVEMENT OR WHILE
INVESTIGATION TAKES PLACE)
1 TO 4 WEEKS

DISMISSAL

fore, it's only natural to put off doing something which isn't urgent. One of those less-than-urgent items is to review the progress of a probationary employee.

Linda was hired for a three-month probationary period. At the end of each thirty-day period her manager needs to review her performance, tell her how she's doing, and make recommendations for the future. Her manager, however, is very busy and she puts off doing the review. Suddenly, the whole three months have elapsed. Linda's probationary period is ending. It's time to decide whether or not to keep her. Her manager looks at her performance. It's terrible. She hasn't done one thing right. In fact, she's made a nuisance of herself and hindered other workers. "Get rid of her!" is the manager's decision. But Linda protests. "It's unfair. No one told me I wasn't doing what was expected. No one reviewed my work. How was I to know? If I had been told, I would have done better."

The manager didn't do her work. She didn't follow procedure and she doesn't have any documentation. She's probably stuck with Linda, at least for the present.

Probationary workers must be given reviews, criticism, reprimands, warnings, and possibly even suspensions, just like regular workers. In other words, it can't be a surprise to them if you want to fire them. If it is, then you may not get away with the firing.

FIRING A
CONTRACT EMPLOYEE

Some employees have contracts with an employer. In such cases, the firing practice is somewhat different. Some managers, however, make the error of thinking that the method of firing all employees is identical.

With a contract worker, there is usually only one basic way to fire. It must be shown that the worker is not living up to one or more terms of the contract. This is known as a "contract breaker clause." Even should such a clause exist, it still does not mean the worker can be fired quickly or easily. It may be necessary to show that the poor performance is gross, significant, and major in terms of the contract. This can require a set procedure and documentation.

Often the easiest way out with a contract worker is to wait until the contract expires and then refuse to renew. (*Note:* This section does not concern the contracting with an outside agency or other employer to provide a company with employees, as is sometimes done. It refers only to contracts made directly with individual employees.)

FAILURE TO DISCUSS THE PROBLEM WITH THE WORKER

Sometimes managers will think that simply handing out written reprimands and warnings can be enough. That's usually not the case.

It is important that the manager show a good faith attempt to explain the problem and find a means to a solution with the employee. Simply warning without making the attempt to find a solution is not enough. The worker might actually have a very good reason for not performing. For example, it would be embarrassing at the least to realize after firing someone that the worker was making mistakes in billing because they had a serious, but correctable eyesight problem that they were unaware of or that they were hesitant to address.

FAILURE TO ALLOW SUFFICIENT NOTICE

Although we've been emphasizing this point throughout this chapter, it bears mentioning again. In today's world a manager does not simply walk up and fire a worker without notice, not if that manager wants to keep his or her own job.

Workers have rights and they are protected. To fire a worker, normally a case must be built. An important part of the case is providing sufficient notice so that the worker understands what the problem is and has the opportunity to correct it. If you surprise a worker with a firing, you could be in trouble.

OVERLOOKING SEVERANCE PAY

Severance pay is frowned upon by many managers. Why should they give money to a person being fired for cause?

One reason is that it may keep the person from coming back with a lawsuit. It's not pleasant to think of it as a bribe, but if paying a small amount of money now can avoid paying a large amount of money later (not to mention headaches and time lost), then it may be a good trade.

(*Note:* Some managers get terminated employees to sign a statement that they will not contest the firing in exchange for receiving severance pay. It's not clear whether such agreements are enforceable.)

ACTING OUT OF ANGER

A worker does something wrong, something which really upsets you. You want to resolve the issue and get satisfaction right away. In short, you want revenge. So you storm out and fire the individual.

That's a "No, no!"

Firing is a major decision. It should never be done on the spur of the moment. Take the time to clear your head. Make it your policy never to act until at least twenty-four hours have passed.

Then investigate. Be sure you really know what's happened. Be certain you have the right person and that they really did or didn't do what you think.

Then *follow procedure* and *document!*

It's the procedure and documentation which will protect *you* in the end.

TASK 15
FIRING: DISMISSAL INTERVIEW

Sorry, you don't work here anymore.

Manager firing
for the first time

The hardest part of firing is undoubtedly the dismissal itself. The real stress point comes when the manager informs the employee, often face-to-face, that the job is terminated.

In this chapter we'll see how to dismiss correctly. We'll also look into the emotional distress that often accompanies job termination.

EMOTIONAL DISTRESS ON THE MANAGER'S PART

Managers often feel enormous guilt about firing. The manager may feel as though he or she is ruining the worker's life. A job is, after all, a livelihood. Firing takes away another person's means of earning a living. In a very real sense it could mean putting that person out onto the street.

What if they can't find other employment? What if the act of firing is the final straw that turns them into a derelict? In the greatest extreme, what if next week's paper reports that they committed suicide—is the manager responsible?

Such can be the feelings of a manager who has to fire an employee. There's a germ of truth in these feelings, which is what makes them so compelling. But there is the other side of the picture that managers need to focus on.

WHO'S RESPONSIBLE

An employee is equal to yourself in every way except for the job position you hold. In other words, the employee is an equal human being—a person responsible for what happens in his or her life.

If you have followed a firing procedure (as detailed in Task 14), then before dismissal you will have made every effort to inform the employee of the problem and to offer an opportunity to correct it. Ultimately, therefore, the reason you are firing is because the worker has chosen not to change, not to correct the problem.

To put it another way, if you have been fair in following your firing procedure (going from criticism to warnings), then it is the worker's actions which resulted in the firing. He or she knew that dismissal was a consequence (both from oral and written warnings). Yet, the worker chose not to take corrective steps. The worker, therefore, is the one who is ultimately responsible for the dismissal.

Accepting responsibility is what being a mature human being is all about. If you are to accept your responsibility as a manager, you must be willing to fire workers who don't perform. Similarly workers must also be able to accept the consequences of their lack of performance.

DISMISSAL ISN'T THE END OF THE WORLD

A dismissed worker will most likely find another job. And the new job may be more suited to that person's skills, talents, and temperament. In other words, you may actually be doing someone a favor by dismissing that person from a job he or she can't handle. Remember, people are resilient. The worker will usually rebound and perhaps be better off for what happened in the long run.

When your job calls for you to dismiss, accept your responsibility and do it unflinchingly. Dismiss the worker, get it over with, then move on. Don't ever look over your shoulder and wonder.

EMOTIONAL DISTRESS
ON THE PART OF
THE DISMISSED EMPLOYEE

It's important to understand that as bad as you may feel when dismissing someone, the real emotional pain is on the part of the worker. Don't expect the worker to comfort you. Rather, you may need to comfort them.

Some dismissed employees have described their feelings at the time they were terminated as a little bit like being told they had a terminal illness. Much research has been done into the emotions involved with dying and it is generally accepted that there are at least four basic steps that people go through. People who are fired often experience the same phases:

1. *Surprise:* There is almost always surprise at the actual dismissal even if the person knew they were going to be fired.

2. *Argument:* The person may laugh or kid trying to get you to say that it really isn't true, that it's a big joke. They may try to talk you out of it.

3. *Anger/Depression:* These are really two sides of the same thing. Anger comes first. The dismissed worker may suddenly blame you and even shout and rage. Then, sometimes very soon afterward, the person may redirect their anger at themselves. Self-directed anger, however, tends to be expressed as depression. They may slump down and sink into a depressed state.

4. *Acceptance:* Ultimately the fired worker will accept the dismissal and will move on to finding a new job.

The entire course of this four-stage emotional reaction typically takes several days. Some managers, however, have reported seeing many of the steps passed through in just the few minutes that it takes to handle a dismissal meeting.

When the worker experiences this emotional distress, it is important to understand there isn't a whole lot you can do. Comforting is helpful. However, the worker may simply have to go through some emotional distress until he or she accepts the dismissal. If you recognize that what's happening is relatively normal, you shouldn't panic or otherwise be thrown by it.

THE TIME OF DISMISSAL

In the United States probably more than half of all workers fired are dismissed late Friday afternoon. There's a good reason for this.

A dismissal should be a clean break. There is nothing worse than dismissing someone and then having them hang around the office for a few days or weeks. That person becomes the living dead. Other workers don't know what to say to the dismissed employee. You can't really give the person orders because he or she doesn't work for you anymore. To have a dismissed person remain on the job for a period of time is embarrassing and potentially damaging to the morale and productivity of the remaining workers.

Some managers are concerned about having dismissed employees work off termination or severance pay. Don't consider it. Dismissed employees will give you 10 percent of their attention, if that. As soon as they are fired, their full-time job becomes finding other employment, not finishing up work for you.

All of which is to say that ideally a dismissal will be a clean break. The employee is terminated, picks up his or her final check, cleans out the desk or work station, and permanently leaves. (Some employers provide out-placement services—desk, phone, and even secretarial help for the fired worker. This is all fine, but be sure these services are somewhere other than the regular workplace. If you provide these services, set up the dismissed worker in a separate building or location where he or she won't come into contact with other workers.)

The reason that Friday afternoon is most often selected is because it is the end of the week and the dismissed worker normally would have the next two days off. These two days are an excellent cooling off period. During that time the dismissed worker can transition through the emotional steps of the dismissal. A worker dismissed on a Friday afternoon is least likely to provoke a scene or to show up the next work day to badger the rest of the staff.

A worker dismissed at 4:45 can usually clean out his or her desk and finish up after the other workers have gone home. Again it avoids embarrassing situations.

Some managers are concerned about the increased shock to the worker of getting dismissed right before the weekend. True, this can be emotionally trying for the worker who may have anticipated a calm weekend. But dismissal is going to be shocking anytime. At least on Friday night the shock is entirely the dismissed worker's and isn't spread among the remainder of the workforce.

THE WRITTEN DISMISSAL

The worker should be given a written dismissal notice. It should state clearly the name of the person, the name of the company, the name of the job and, most important, that the person has been terminated. Some notices go on to indicate the reason for termination.

The importance of the written notice is that it adds to the documentation. With written notice, the worker can't claim that he or she misunderstood. It's there to see in black and white.

Dismissal notices also have their dark side. Some managers use the dismissal notice as the vehicle for dismissing the worker—the "pink slip" with Friday's paycheck. Dismissing a worker by using *only* a written notice is wrong ethically, practically, and economically. From an ethical viewpoint, the worker is entitled to be told, face to face. It's only common decency to do so.

From a practical perspective, getting only a written dismissal notice may be confusing. The worker may have some practical questions to ask. The manager has gone home and there's no one to give answers. So the worker shows up next Monday and an embarrassing meeting ensues. Rather than avoiding confrontation, the technique may actually provoke an even more difficult confrontation.

Finally, getting only a written dismissal notice may anger the worker to the point of taking some kind of retaliation against the company. A lawsuit, even if won by the company, can be a time-consuming and expensive experience. From an economic viewpoint, it's usually far better to give the worker a few minutes of personal time.

THE DISMISSAL MEETING

The dismissal meeting is when you tell the worker that he or she is fired and may hand them the dismissal notice and, usually, a final paycheck. There is no way in which this is not going to be a difficult meeting for both of you. But it need not be a long meeting. And it can provide the worker the opportunity to make a final statement.

It can be a positive meeting for you. It can clue you in on whether or not the worker plans to pursue a wrongful discharge claim. You can also sometimes gain valuable insights into your own management techniques. Workers may say things at the dismissal meeting that they were afraid of saying before. You may come to realize things you are doing badly that you never before saw.

Some managers come to dismissal meetings with a number of items to cushion the blow. Besides the last paycheck, the manager may be in a position to discuss severance pay. (Sometimes it is advantageous to get the worker to agree here on a specific amount of severance pay.) Or the manager may be able to offer a temporary continuance of medical benefits (frequently an important item to dismissed workers). Finally, the manager may be able to temporarily offer outplacement, desk space, phone, and even secretarial service to help the dismissed worker locate a new job.

THE MEETING ITSELF

There are seven good rules that a manager should keep in mind when going into a dismissal meeting. These should help keep things on the right track.

1. *Don't have a dismissal meeting when you're angry.* Be sure you're calm and can think clearly.

2. *Don't keep the point of the meeting a secret.* As soon as the worker comes in, tell the person that he or she is dismissed. Yes, you can shake hands and exchange a "Hello, how are you." Then state the reason

you are meeting. Any delay shows weakness and indecision on your part.

3. *Don't discuss the person.* You're not a therapist. It's not your position to tell people what's wrong with them or what they need to do to get better. They could be outraged if you try to.

4. *Do sympathize, don't apologize.* You can sincerely say you're sorry that things didn't work out. You can empathize and say that you can understand how difficult this must be for them. But don't apologize. Apologies make the worker think that you are in some way to blame. Apologies make it sound like it's your fault that the person got fired. It's not your fault. At this stage of the game, finding fault is pointless. You are doing your job and you have nothing to apologize for.

5. *Don't rehash the problem.* The point of the meeting is to tell the worker he or she is *dismissed.* It is *not* to go over your firing decision. If you rehash the worker's problem, you can open a Pandora's box of whining, promising to improve in the future, and cajoling as the worker tries to get you to reconsider the dismissal. Your mind is made up and nothing will change it. The decision is final.

6. *When things get tough, talk about the future.* The worker does have a future beyond the confines of your direction and your company. Point that out and try to get the worker future-directed. This dismissal may actually turn out to be a plus for the worker, if it moves him or her in a positive direction. Many workers who knew the current job wasn't working out will admit this, and may themselves turn the meeting into a positive event. Looking forward will help both you and the worker to get past the present moment.

7. *Listen carefully.* Besides emotional distress, is the worker giving clues about taking possible retaliatory ac-

tion? What kind? Is there anything you can do or say now that will head it off? Also, is the worker saying something valuable about your management technique? Are you paying attention so that you can improve yourself?

A typical dismissal meeting takes about ten minutes. If you see that it's taking longer, simply end it. There really isn't a whole lot to say, and dragging things out can get messy for everyone concerned.

AFTER THE MEETING

After the dismissal meeting it's a good idea to write up a brief statement of what transpired. This is part of the documentation and should be placed in the worker's permanent file.

CONCLUSION

Management is 90 percent hard work,
10 percent inspiration,
and 100 percent common sense.

A company V.P. on
her retirement day.

I f you've read through all the tasks in this book, you may find yourself drawing an unforseen conclusion: regardless of the task you need to perform, it may seem that if you use common sense you'll come out all right.

Yes, common sense, in fact, is the key to dealing with most management situations. That doesn't mean, however, that you should run blindly into each problem trusting to your good judgment to bail you out. It may be that lack of experience, emotional upset (such as being fearful, hostile, or angry), or not fully appreciating the totality of the problem, could do you in. Rather, a cautious approach is suggested.

When you have a problem in management, use the following strategy. You may find it works even when common sense is nowhere to be found:

STOP!

Take a break. Leave the room or the building. Go for a walk. Take the time to cool down and gain perspective. Look at the big picture and see where the "small" problem of the moment fits in.

DEFINE THE PROBLEM

What *exactly* is wrong? No, it's not that you have a "lazy" worker. It's not that you have an unsurmountable difficulty. Cut your problem down to size. Is it the need to "criticize" a worker? Should you give a "reprimand?" Are you in need of "documentation?" Is knowing what to ask in the "interview" the trouble?" Put a name on that problem and you'll be able to handle it.

TREAT IT AS A TASK

Once you have the problem defined, think of it as simply a task to be completed. As a first step, refer to the tasks in this book. They offer fifteen solid solutions to the most common problems in managing people.

THE TASK APPROACH

We call this the "Task Approach" to management. We have found it works as an effective strategy in every management situation we've run into. We sincerely hope you will find that it also works for you!

The authors offer management counseling for specific problems. They also provide management training through seminars for companies. Contact "Task Management Answers," Box 7803, Westlake, California 91359-7803.

INDEX

ABOUT THE AUTHORS

Robert Irwin is the author of more than fifteen books on investing and real estate, including *The New Mortgage Game* and *Wealth Builders*. He lives in California with his wife and coauthor Rita Wolenik, a management consultant for business and government agencies. She has been an elementary and college teacher, counselor, and administrator.